Our Voices

Our Voices

Diana Radovan

Matador
Unit E2 Airfield Business Park,
Harrison Road, Market Harborough,
Leicestershire. LE16 7UL
Tel: 0116 279 2299
Email: books@troubador.co.uk
Web: www.troubador.co.uk/matador
Twitter: @matadorbooks

ISBN 978 1803130 736

British Library Cataloguing in Publication Data.
A catalogue record for this book is available from the British Library.

Printed and bound by CPI Group (UK) Ltd, Croydon, CR0 4YY
Typeset in 12pt Adobe Jenson Pro by Troubador Publishing Ltd, Leicester, UK

Matador is an imprint of Troubador Publishing Ltd

"It is an undeniable fact that everything passes – animals, plants, ideas, beliefs, civilizations, anything that has a glimmer of life. All die and decay, and from the ruins and detritus springs new life, both similar and dissimilar to that preceding it."

Karen Bayly in *Fortitude*,
published by Mary Celeste Press in 2019

Contents

Foreword

MOST OF THE words in *Our Voices* initially belonged to Diana Radovan.

Some of the words in this book were first written in Romanian by her mother Mia (Maria) and her mother's father, Iuliu, whose voices were silenced by political oppression, illness, and premature death. They are included in this book as Diana's translation.

Our Voices is dedicated to them.

All images included in *Our Voices* were taken by Diana, by her father (used with his permission), or originate from other sources in her personal collection.

Now, the words and images *in Our Voices* only partially belong to Diana and her ancestors. They mostly belong to this book's readers.

Prologue

The Girl behind the Curtain

ONCE, THERE WAS a little girl. The girl liked to read books more than anything else. She dreamed of becoming a writer. One day. But writers were not welcome in her country, which was known as *Republica Socialistă România (RSR)*. The censors would cut off their words. They would either take them out completely or replace them with other, less harmful words. For instance, the word *geamantan* (EN "suitcase") was really bad. It made people think of absurd things like traveling, like leaving their home country. And the country could not be left, not alive, at least. So why put such nonsense into people's heads to begin with?

There was a big long river bordering the South of that country, far beyond the curtain that was said to be of iron. They called that river *Dunărea* (EN "the Danube"). Whoever tried to swim across it at night, to the shore of another country, which was known as Yugoslavia, would get shot and killed. The springs of the Danube were far away, on the other side of the Iron Curtain, in a country called *Germania* (EN "Germany"), where dogs were rumored to run around with pretzels on their tails.

Words were dangerous, they made people dream of impossible things. So why write them down or say them out loud in the first place? And yet, on some days, despite everything, the girl still dreamed. On other days, she wrote on her typewriter. But there were also days, as she grew up, when the weight of all the words she could not say out loud was so heavy that it kept her imprisoned in her bed and her own thoughts. The thoughts were often about how unworthy she was. Unworthy of making her voice heard, being loved, or being successful in life.

On some days, this girl is my mother. On other days, she is me. But there are also days when she could be anyone else, on either side of that heavy curtain that is nowadays rumored to exist no more. She is an embryo; she is 3, 5, 35, 72. Her name is Mia, Diana, Ella, you.

Voice I – Diana

(Childhood; Tree of Life)

The Family and the Tree

In first grade, in the spring of 1989, I am asked in school to make a drawing of my family. Our teacher invites my aunt, my mother's sister, who is a child psychologist, to come to our classroom on that particular day. Thus, it is my aunt who asks us to make that drawing, so that each of us can get a psychological assessment. In my drawing, I place myself between my parents. Next to my mother stands her mother. And next to my father – my uncle, my cousin, and my aunt. My grandparents from my father's side and my maternal grandfather aren't there. Those of us who are present – we are all holding hands.

My aunt also asks us to draw a tree, on another sheet of paper. Mine is in the middle of the page and its trunk is at its center; the tree's branches and leaves are undefined, but they spread in all directions, everywhere, everywhere, like arms that want to hug the entire world, as if there cannot be enough white space to fill.

Voices Rising – Worship

25 December 1989

The Dictator is dead. The shoemaker is dead. This is what the TV says. They shot him and his wife right on Christmas. They showed the trial on TV but not the shooting. The dictator was our president. He was our beloved father. Until now, we had never talked about him as a dictator. I had no clue he was a shoemaker.

The TV now runs for more than 2 hours a day. Will they now stop shooting? Will we still need to worry about hiding in the basement if the terrorists come? Will we? Will they?

15 October 1989

I am a so-called Detachment Commander. I am a pioneer and a proud member of the Romanian Communist Party. Nobody wears the yellow belt with more pride than me. At least not in Timișoara, where I live. I am the only one in my classroom who gets to wear it. I am in charge of 40 little pioneers, including myself. I should be proud. I should not be so shy. Our president does not like shy children. Children must work to create the future. My parents are engineers. That is a good occupation. It serves the goals of the Party. I am 7. If I say the wrong thing, Mom and Dad may go to prison. There are things we never talk about at home. It's better for me not to know certain things, but I can still hear my parents whisper.

As Detachment Commander of pioneers of the Romanian Communist Party, it is my task to:

- check that all pioneers in my classroom cut their nails and do their homework
- make sure there is silence in the classroom when our teacher isn't there
- give the tone of our national anthem each morning, in front of Nicolae Ceaușescu's portrait, which reigns majestically just above the blackboard.

He is our president, our beloved father. The photo is black and white, like the images in our TV at home. The bottom TV is for sound and the upper one for images. When the top TV doesn't work, Grandma slaps it. If it still does not work, she slaps it again, harder. Then we are all happy. I watch Yugoslavian cartoons with audio, even if I don't know Yugoslavian.

Of all my tasks, the last one is my favorite, because I love singing. When I sing, I don't feel shy. I also love:

- writing poems about butterflies and stars
- learning new German words, although once, at the public German *Kindergarten*, an inspector said we needed to sing and recite poems in Romanian much more often than in German
- going with my dad to his art studio and painting the door together
- playing with my cousin's dog Ajax and with my best friend Alina
- not wearing socks in summer
- making lists like this one.

Before becoming a pioneer, I was a hawk. Sometimes, I still feel like I'm just a baby hawk. *Mama*'s baby hawk.

I don't know what I want to be when I grow up, I must think more about that. All the other kids in my classroom know; they are real pioneers. It's not good for a Commander not to know. I am the tallest and youngest one in my classroom. Maybe that's why I'm so shy. Commanders should not be shy and weak. Self-confidence and determination should be their main character traits. The advice I get when I am handed my red tie is: "Have more confidence in your own abilities." At the pioneering ceremony, the text behind us says: "The rhythmic fulfillment of the plan is the patriotic duty of all communists and people of labor."

15 November 1989

"Antibaby, antibaby!" is what the *bişniţari* (EN "black market dealers") are screaming at the marketplace. They usually sell chocolate from Yugoslavia. *Eurocrem* and *Cipiripi*. My dad's name is Cipri(an). I sometimes call him Cipiripi. We have a Yugoslavian family name but we are Socialist Romanians! I am here with *mama* and I tell her I want *antibaby* too. She tells me that *antibaby* is not chocolate and is not for children, but not more. I don't know why, but I feel defeated.

17 December 1989

I am at my grandmother's place. I call her *Mica* (EN "The Little One"), but that's not her real name. Her real name is Maria Lucreția, like *mama*'s. I am coloring a book with many sleeping kittens in it. The glazed stove in my parents' room – which we heat up with wood and carbon – exploded last night, so now all my kittens are a bit gray. I cried a lot about it last night but now it's sorta OK. I am eating *Eurocrem* and *Cipiripi*. Soon, *Moș Crăciun* will come. At school I have to constantly remind myself to call him *Moș Gerilă*. I'd better not get them mixed up. *Mama* gets to Mica's early from work. Dad too. This is unusual. "Let's go home," they say. "There has been a lot going on. Broken windows. Demonstrations. Angry people. And shootings. Let's go home," they say. "Before it's too late."

21 December 1989

We are watching TV. The president is talking to the crowd. He is raising his hand. "Dear comrades and friends," he says, as always. But the comrades are howling. They won't listen. The camera moves. There are tanks in the streets. The dictator and his wife are no longer there. The camera moves again. The people on the tanks are screaming: "The Army is with you!"

22 December 1989

There is shooting day and night. We cannot leave the house. I cannot draw in my coloring books. The sound of my crayons on paper is driving Dad crazy. "Stop it," he says. It reminds him of the shootings, from the last days, but also from WWII. *Mica* calls us. She tells us stories. People found dead in their beds. Bullets passing through walls, into people's heads. They found munition in her neighbor's backyard. "We must be careful with what we say on the phone," Dad says. "We must keep sealing our homes."

23 December 1989

They are shooting from the tower of the Catholic Church in our neighborhood. From the tower of the Orthodox Cathedral in the city center. Alina and her mom visit us, so that Alina and I can talk and play. When they take a shooting break, she and her mom go home. "Tomorrow," I tell her before she leaves. "Maybe tomorrow we can play some more."

On TV, they are still saying: "The Army is with you!" There are still many tanks on the streets. And I can't tell who is shooting: is it the terrorists or the Army? If the Army is with us, why are they shooting?

I've been going to bed early since the shootings started. At 6:30 pm at the latest, right after we watch the evening news. I want to sleep through it if the terrorists come and Mom has to carry me in her arms into the basement. I want to be asleep when I die. Or worse, if I live and Mom and Dad die. I don't want to be brought up by terrorists.

24 December 1989

We are putting up the Christmas tree and hanging the glass globes. The pink ones are my favorite. We don't have any chocolate to hang this year.

But we are lucky. Before the shootings, there were unexpected sales of chicken, bananas, and oranges. I lined up in front of the store several times, with my parents, my grandma, and all their neighbors. Having children standing in line with you is good. Then you get more.

We still have enough oil, butter and sugar from our monthly ration. Dad goes out to buy bread. That is the only thing we still need. At home with my mom, I listen to songs on the radio, about grown-up love. I just love Angela Similea's voice and lyrics! Oh, how I also want that kind of love one day! With Dad gone for bread, I can finally draw in my coloring book again. When I do that, I feel safe, or at least I used to, before the shootings.

They're shooting again. I don't want to think about my dad being in danger or dying. I stop coloring and just listen to the radio. Actually, the love song on the radio kinda sucks.

29 December 1989

The *Front of the National Salvation* – including Ion Iliescu and Petre Roman – are on TV day and night. Mom and I are both falling in love with Petre Roman. "He's so photogenic," she says. I want it to snow but Mom says going sleighing wouldn't be safe yet anyway.

10 January 1990

I've never had such a long winter vacation. I have done all my homework assignments, for both Romanian and Maths. It's the first day back at school. The photo of the dictator is gone, and so are my singing and Detachment Commander days. I am afraid to be alone in the bathroom when I pee. What if someone is watching, listening?

We get so-called help from France. *Marmeladă*. Used toys and clothes from rich children. Pencils. Drawing books. It looks like the stuff they got bored of, so they sent it to us instead of throwing it all away. I hadn't known we needed help; that we were poor; that our president was an evil dictator. I thought he was our loving father. I thought we were the richest country in the world. That all families in the world ate what they got with their monthly ration, just like us.

I don't know anything anymore. It is now OK again to go to Alina's house and play. Alina writes labels on all the paper bags she finds in the kitchen: *bomboane comuniste* (EN "communist candy"). We laugh. Alina is always so funny. I somehow survived to this day. I still go to bed a 6:30 pm. I don't want to grow older.

22 February 1990

On TV, they are showing the Dictator's home. While the country lived in poverty, he lived in a palace. Even the toilettes are golden. They are interviewing his grown-up children. People are burning their Communist Party membership cards on TV. I don't know if Mom and Dad burnt theirs. I haven't seen them do it.

God and the Dictator are no longer competing against each other. His Sanctity, the Mitropolitan of the Romanian Orthodox Church, is on TV and says: "The Church has always been a symbol of resistance. The Holy Trinity has always been on our side," he says.

There are Christian cartoons on TV now. Stories from the Bible, adapted for children. I'd never heard about the Bible before. There are also movies, with foreign actors. They all speak in English, with Romanian subtitles.

25 April 1990

After *mama* said I can't marry Petre Roman, I'm no longer in love with him. Now I have a crush on Jesus. "Can I marry Jesus?" I ask her. "No," she says. "Now eat your marmalade-and-margarine bread. Eat all of it and drink your vitamins. You're so skinny!"

I am skinny and I am almost always sick. This is why I need vitamins. And *Polidin* shots from my aunt, to boost my immune system. In Romania all children are skinny. This is the first time ever that I am eating German *Rama* margarine sold in a store in Romania! Dad bought *Rama* from the store! I love *Rama* so much that I can eat it without anything, every day, even without bread.

5 May 1990

Easter vacation is beyond over. Above the blackboard hangs a photo of Mother Mary holding Baby Jesus, like the one Mom still hides in her wardrobe, except that this one's much bigger. "Come on, children," says the teacher, "let's stand up and pray." This won't go unpunished, but I will not stand up. I will not pray.

My Voice (I)

I dream that I'm dancing; this dance never ends and I dance with you inside the waves and insist that they should not wash the dirt away. The small eyes of paradise lie hidden inside a walnut; in-here, a fairy is sewing a wedding dress, from butterfly silk. These are my hands without skin, my eyes without sight, my feet bleeding, I am the little mermaid, I am waiting, it is up to you how you wish to shape the reality of my dreams. Here are the cherry stains on mine and my grandmother's aprons, here is where I bruised my knee falling from the swing, and I'd put on white stockings so that nobody would see the bruises, then I'd scratch the bruise and cry at the sight of blood. I'd cry out of anything, the rain terrified me, the first green rain when I was 2 years old and our terrace was flooded. The brown river on my street when rain would pour angrily with thunder and lightning in summer, under my one and only acacia tree that would spread its arms and leaves up to my bedroom window, before it was hit by lightning and they chopped it down, so that it wouldn't fall over our home, which was right under the roof of an old house built on shaky grounds. The whole house would shake when cars would pass by on the street. It was summer and I wanted to keep coloring my books, while the entire world shuddered. Books fell over me in my sleep during an earthquake. I would wash the grains in 7 waters. I would wash my dolls, even when I had hepatitis. My eyes were yellow and my hands wet. My first marriage proposal when I was 3 years old. I was walking with him in the park that we called forest. He kissed one of my eyelids first, then the other. He placed my hairpin back where it belonged, but my hair was short, too short, like my dress. My mother was ill, but loved me. People seemed mean at times, and I wanted to be somebody else, in another time and place. I wanted to turn into Rhoda and swing my boats at the sea shore...dance with the fireflies and the *night butterflies,* as I'd call them, and follow them into the darkness. No! I am the light of a morning. I drink the nectar of each morning, with the flowers, the birds, and the bees. With the *day butterflies*. I, I. And you. You?

Mica

My Grandfather, the Living Ghost

In the middle of the dining room, at my grandmother's and aunt's place, my grandfather's portrait reigns. He has long been dead. He died in 1964. I was born in 1982. His wife, *Mica,* is still alive. She was 28 years old when my mother was born and my grandfather was 41 back then.

Throughout my childhood, *Mica* cooks for us every morning, like a ritual, like she also used to do for her husband once they got married. She does it mostly in silence, without taking up much space, despite her broad hips and shoulders. *Mica* is the only grandparent I ever met after being born. All my other grandparents had long been dead, the longest time her husband, *bunicu' Iuliu.*

There are many stories about him in our family, more often about his death than about his life. He looks a bit like Mihai Eminescu, our national poet, in that painting. A tall forehead, dark hair sliding towards the back of his head, a long face with well-defined cheekbones, the kind of features that my mother inherited, but not me, and thick, ripe lips. My grandfather was a poet too, like me. And a notary. But there's also something that we don't often talk about. I know not to ask questions.

—∞—

Before I was born, have we all met somewhere else? Were we already a family up in Heaven? Did we write poems together in Heaven? And up there, could I hear the sound of *Bunicu'* Iuliu's voice? See him smile? Know what it means to be held by him? But if religion is a lie, isn't Heaven a lie too?

—∞—

As I grow up, my mother and my grandmother tell me stories. Except that they are not stories. These things that they tell me, they are real. The way they remember them, at least. Real pieces of our family history. But they are like a puzzle. And so many pieces of the puzzle are missing. We look at old photo albums. Sepia photos, in which the colors are fading away. My grandmother's wedding. My mother's first day of school. There are several images from my childhood that persist in my memory. Like slices of reality that could be added to our photography collection.

—∞—

Whenever cousins of my mother visit us at my grandmother's place, we eat. My grandmother and aunt always cook for all our relatives. And then we talk. No. They talk, I listen. They talk about everyone in our extended family, where they are, how they are doing, what is happening in their lives.

And we always end up talking about my grandfather, but each time, I feel like certain things are left out, on purpose, because I am there, a child who is not supposed to know everything. I am a quiet child, used to being among grown-ups. My cousin is 9 years older than me and he is the closest person to my age in our whole family.

So I listen a lot. I keep quiet, listen, and observe. They think I am shy, but I keep on learning and listening. I listen to the story of how my grandfather's brother killed himself by pushing a sharp knife through his heart. Of how this man's grandson has schizophrenia.

Year by year, the grown-ups tell me more things. But there is always this silence, this mystery, this sadness. Things that I can tell they do not wish to discuss in my presence. My family – at least my mother's side of the family – seems to be defined by my grandfather's absence. This is why he is my grandfather, the living ghost.

The Garden

It is in *Mica*'s garden that I learned that sometimes you need to fight your neighbors. Although her garden was in the city and not in the countryside, I had everything I needed here: a swing where I would twirl and read, and then untwirl; trees with ripe fruit across all the summer months (cherry, sour cherry, apricot, peach, fig, and others), grapes (of 3 different colors no less), strawberries, and tomatoes. I had time to play with other kids or by myself, a dog, stairs to jump on and off. I could be by myself while also knowing I was in a safe space, one of magical daydreaming, of eating ripe or not so ripe fruit and fresh vegetables, a haven of protection and attention, one where both nature and humans would hold me gently when I wanted to be held and, at the same time, one where I could be free and fully myself when I wanted it. Free to run, to dream, to read, to twirl.

The *Magnetofon*

There's a voice on the *magnetofon*. And then another one. It's my maternal grandmother and my paternal grandfather, talking to each other. Everyday things. My father is the one recording them. It is 1988. The recording is from 10 years ago. Back then, I wasn't around.

I am only 6 years old. I will start school soon. *Mica* is still alive. She is old but she can still take care of me, of us. My other grandfather, my father's father, who used to be a primary school teacher, died soon after my father did this recording. He died of a bad heart. Without the recording, I would have never known the sound of his voice. When he died, my mother lost her first pregnancy. Two years later, I was born. My grandfathers aren't human beings, they're human stories.

Smell

Throughout my childhood, my grandmother smelled like old cotton sheets that had spent too much time drying outside in the sun, as if someone had forgotten them there, as if she had forgotten to leave the house and go out and pick herself up; the folds stayed and were many. Many things were in plain sight in her garden, growing wild. Other things were in her basement, like the wooden barrel from which she would squeeze *Sauerkraut* for our lunch, or her hens, whose heads she would chop off without hesitation with a big old axe. I would watch her do it. Other things were in drawers or not even physically there, unspoken of. Sometimes she would fall asleep in her chair, forgetting herself, forgetting that I was there, forgetting that she was supposed to watch over me. Then she would wake up and cook.

—~~—

I've always liked strange smells as a child. I loved the smell of *terpinol* at my father's studio, it was what he'd use for his paintings. Just like I loved the smell of white paint at home, be it for doors or walls. My parents and especially my uncle seemed to always be painting something. Something always needed repairing, things were continuously broken or out of place. Repairing, transforming, sewing, cropping.

My mother, aunt, and grandmother all used to sew so-called *macrameuri*. They would sew pillows, table cloths, and much more. Damaged socks, anything with holes in it. They would croché, my mother especially. My aunt and grandmother would knit. Sweaters, scarfs, mittens, pullovers, the full set. Cook for the winter. *Zacuscă*. *Marmeladă*. *Murături*. Nothing was missing. In the 80s, it was important to store stuff because you never knew when you could be left with nothing. You could not buy fresh fruit and vegetables in winter and you never knew how much heating you'd get and whether you could still cook or not, so you had to be prepared.

Later, in the early 90s, my aunt would sell the *macrameuri* at the market in Serbia, crossing the border with them under her skirt. It is how she saved enough money to buy my cousin's first color TV, a Blaupunkt from Germany. It was the time of the Deutsche Mark.

When my grandmother died and her house was sold, it was sold in Deutsche Mark too.

—⁓—

Smell. My dad's painting studio on *Strada Ceahlău*. The long and winding road from his studio to the old bathroom on the hallway. Wood that is half-rotten and *trozneşte*. Keys, lots of keys. Mom and Dad. Safety. I haven't been there in a long time. Cold, endless cold in winter. Sometimes mice. Pee smell. And still, a smell like home.

—⁓—

In 2016, I keep remembering it from afar. I don't know how I will be without this place, without my dad, one day. I haven't been there in a long time. This place is like a storage room for ancient souls. Like an entrance to another time. Somewhere deep in the enigma of my childhood. An evocation of the past. Even back then, the place was old. Now it seems to belong to another world, especially from here, far away. Somewhere, this place still exists in the present.

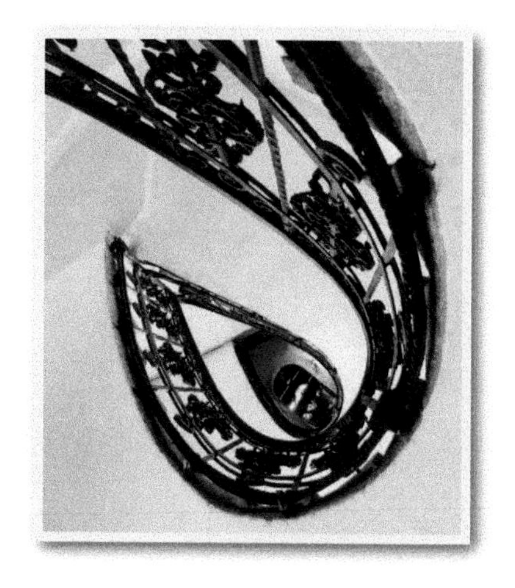

The Room

It is 1987. I wake up in cold sweats in the middle of the night, screaming, half-asleep. I don't remember the details of my half-awakening; they come from my dad in flashbacks, days later, but I remember the restlessness, the tiredness, the terror. I do remember the recurrent dreams. Someone interrogating me in a dark room. There is nobody and nothing else there in the darkness (although this room is in our home) except the wolf, and the constant pee-like smell of my fear. It is this fear that prevents me from opening the door, from moving into my room, where I'd be safe, or safer. All I have to do is open the locked door between them, but I can't move.

—w—

The fear is my own and it isn't. The dark room where the wolf would take me each night to interrogate me is also my favorite room in my parents' house. Even at daytime, it doesn't get direct sunlight, but it is the room where most of the books in our house are. It is a place of evil at night and good at daytime. A place where I'd seek refuge on hot summer days and celebrate my birthday.

—w—

Another recurrent dream in my childhood:

I am being followed.
"You have no right to kill me!"

I scream and I run,
But the man in black whose face I cannot see
Shoots towards me anyway.
He misses.
I am searching for my keys,
I run and unlock the door our house.
I run, there are many stairs,
And even more doors to unlock.

And then I wake up,
Wake up!
Wake up!
Wake up!

There's only the endless darkness
And a cold, cold sweat.

I am almost awake now.
Almost awake.
Almost awake.
Almost awake.

Am I safe here?
I feel nothing.

I Remember Black (I)

My great aunt Feli (Ofelia) is dead, it is 1992, I am 10 years old, and I am heading towards the cemetery with my parents to a sort of show they put on when people die, which, I am told, goes by the name of "funeral." I know this is supposed to be a sad moment, but I am very curious to see how things go, I have never attended such a ceremony before, and I've never really known Aunt Feli very well, nor liked her very much. All my memories of her are like this: whenever we pay her a visit, she is lying in bed, complaining over how much everything in her body is aching, my dad is talking to her, but I am not really listening to their conversation. I keep on sneezing from the eternal smell of *naftalină* (moth) in her room. At my age, I know a thing or two about the world, including words like "eternal" and *naftalină*. She was my grandfather's sister.

My parents are wearing black clothes and I wonder how they can tolerate the heat, it is mid-August and the sun is burning-hot. We are having a torrid summer this year here in my home town, 35 degrees Celsius in the shade! I am not wearing black, my parents say that black is inappropriate for a child, although, in my opinion, I am not exactly what you'd call a child anymore. But of course, they do not bother to ask for my opinion very often, although saying things like "a person your age" would have sounded so much better than "a child"! But even at my advanced age, I still enjoy jumping on the way to the cemetery in my new blue dress with pretty flowers on it, I just love the way it twirls, here I am, in all my beauty, with my matching blue sandals, and my pretty pink broach on my pretty white collar.

As we approach the cemetery, *mama* tells me to stop doing that, as it is, again, not appropriate to do such things, not in a cemetery, at least, and especially not while going to someone's funeral. Whatever, grown-ups can drive me so crazy sometimes, and today I am not in the mood to take a stand and try to make my point, loud and clear! I know this cemetery, I come here with *mama* quite often, it's been one of our weekend activities for many years now. We go to Great-grandma's Susana and *Bunicu'* Iuliu's grave, where also my grandma and other members of our family will someday be buried, that is, when they will get sick and old and die, like Aunt Feli.

Mama says that she and *tata Cipri* will have to be buried in another set of graves, behind the chapel, next to an uncle of hers, because there is no more space left for them here; and then there is this other cemetery, where all my dead relatives from my father's side can also be visited on weekends, but we do not go there that often. Those relatives would be Grandma Volumia, Grandpa Vasile, and Aunt Ioana (whose name I also carry: my full name is Diana-Cipriana-Ioana), whose grave no one else from the family ever visits. She was a sort of a weirdo and changed her religion. I do not know any of these dead people, just their faces as they appear in our old family photo albums. There are also some photos of them on the graves, showing them at their weddings; they all look young and beautiful there. Only my Aunt Ioana was loved by no one and died alone, so there is no wedding photo for her. I feel bad for Aunt Ioana, yet sometimes I imagine I am her, she seems so cool and interesting, and even though I do not mention this to my parents, I sometimes still doubt all the stuff I've been taught about

angels and Jesus and God. And the strangest thing is, my parents have to pay money every year to ensure that, on that remote day when they will also die, they'll get to lie down in those graves. I know for a fact that adults can be weird, but don't even let me get started on this one! Paying while you are still alive to make sure you have a place to sleep when you are dead, in what world could that make any sense?!

Anyway, although I don't understand what *mama* means by praying at the graves of all these dead-and-gone people for their immortal souls, I kinda enjoy our little ritual of bringing them flowers and lightning candles for them; sometimes that can be a tough job, as it can get very windy, but we have our own little tricks of dealing with the wind gusts. I wonder where I'll be buried when I die, but I don't want to freak *mama* out with such questions. In fact, I have tried starting this discussion with her before, but she wouldn't even listen to me!

So here we are today, going to this terrific event called FUNERAL. We enter the small chapel where Aunt Feli's corpse is sitting on some sort of narrow white bed, with coins on her eyes (weird!) and Uncle Leon is standing right beside her, caressing her pale face. Suddenly, he starts this strange game, where he keeps on trying to close her mouth with his hand, but that does not seem to work. My dad whispers to me that she died with her mouth open and now it won't get closed anymore. NEVER. Well, not really never, my cousin told me that corpses actually rot in the grave. With him I can talk about certain things without him getting all spooked.

Aunt Feli looks small and waxy. Everyone is sobbing or looking sad and absolutely everyone is wearing black, except for me and a little 4-year old boy, a baby, really! Sadly enough, I don't see any children my own age, with whom I could run around, play, and discuss this strange event.

As 4 men from our extended family (uncles I have never met before) carry the bed (or whatever they call it) with the corpse outside on their shoulders, the priest and 2 other men from the church (who are here mostly to sing from time to time and get some money) start this long and boring ceremony, where they keep on repeating the same things over and over again, about Aunt Feli's immortal soul being taken care of by God, and there is all this stuff about the Father, the Son and the Holy Ghost, and we all keep on making these big crosses with our fingers all over our bodies. I remember doing the same at a wedding ceremony I attended not too long ago. I didn't know weddings and funerals were so alike!

From time to time, some really old ladies (they must be 80 or 90 years old by now) cry like crazy. I myself haven't cried that loud since *Kindergarten*, and I find it very disturbing! I try to cry a little, too, it seems like the appropriate thing to do, under such odd circumstances, but that does not work very well, so I just try my best to look serious and really, really sad. My feet start to ache from all this never-ending standing, and I feel bad thinking about this, but I cannot help it!

The ceremony is almost over now, the last and most difficult part begins, covering Aunt Feli's face with a wooden lid. We all proceed to the grave itself, the men in black use ropes to lower down the little white bed with little, white, pale Aunt Feli, until she is way below the ground, and people throw earth balls over her saying "*Fie-i țărâna ușoară!*" (EN "May her earth be light!").

My head hurts, I have never imagined a funeral to be anything like this! What a strange end to this ritual! Poor people gather around us to receive free food from Aunt Feli's daughters (Rodica and Lia) who are both about *tata*'s age (and twins), and there is even more free food later at their place, but *tata* says: "Let's just go home, that's enough for today, it will only be relatives gossiping about other absent, alive relatives!"

Nevertheless, I do not get it, how can people who are supposedly sad possibly be thinking about food in times like this. *Mama* "explains" it, with her typical argument: "It's tradition!" I am not happy with that, of course, but I leave it at that, for now. I am too tired to argue.

At home, at night, after taking a short nap, I put on my sports clothes and go play outside in the garden. Our neighbor's cat gave birth to 3 little kittens, no more than 3 weeks ago. They have finally opened their eyes and are so adorable! Don't tell anyone, but the black one's my favorite!

I Remember Black (II)

IT IS 1997 and I know more now. I know that my grandfather's death was turned into a lie. Everything is covered up with lies. Then with silence, fear, and decades of waiting. For my grandmother, this mostly means waiting to die, which she eventually does. Before, when I was still a child and my parents would drop me off at her place, she'd often say: "Oh, God, why don't you take me and bring me to Iuli? Take me, please!"

Twelve (I)

It is my father who takes the picture. It is a hot summer day. He always does this. Makes me stand in a certain way, look at him from a certain angle. He won't give up until the image is perfect, as in his mind. He's an artist. I do my best to please him each time but that usually takes forever. Years later, I understand that he's framing and reframing our family script, adjusting our reality as an attempt to stay in control, as everything slips away. Years later, I will reject his script and create my own. But here and now, in 1994, I am 12 and we're in the garden we share with other families. The garden is on the ground floor and we live on the top floor of an old house that my parents and I moved into when I was 2. We often take photos here or on our little top floor terrace. When the film comes to an end, there's a click.

Before 1989, finding film was not easy and back then not everyone owned a camera. Even though we can pay someone to develop colored photos now, we also keep our old traditions. We still develop the black and white photos together in the kitchen on Friday or Saturday nights, after dark. Under the red light.

Even when I was a small child, just a few years old, we would do this, then let the photos sink in solution over night in the bathtub. I would only spend some time with him at the kitchen table with all his devices before I would need to go to bed, because we needed darkness to work but I also needed sleep. And then there would be the red light and all the smells of liquids used to fix images on paper. Vinegar. And more.

Overnight the contrast would sharpen in the bathtub. I remember waking up on a Saturday or Sunday morning and rushing to the bathroom to see the loads of photos on top of one another, sticking to each other, the paper still wet, black and white stills of sequences of moments in our lives. I cannot remember a greater joy than that of those mysterious nights in the dark and the red light when it all seemed magic.

Saturday or Sunday mornings our bathtub would be filled with wet photos ready to be dried and witnessed. I still love waking up on such weekends. I still love these bright mornings when images take a clear shape in our bathtub out of the dark.

My mother is rarely in these photos, and from this year onwards, even less so.

Voice II – Mia

(Flowers in the World)

Mia through Iuliu's Eyes

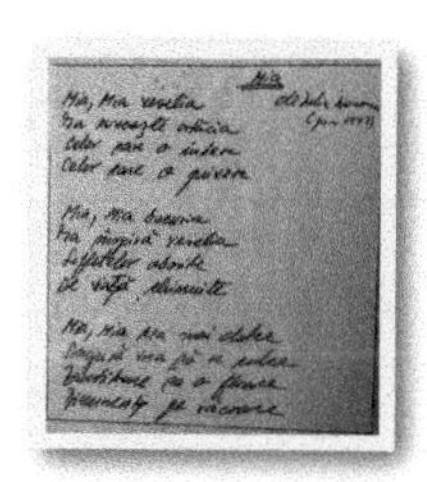

Mia as a small child (possibly 1950).
Poem written in 1947, the year of Mia's birth, by Iuliu Ioanovici,
transcribed in Mia's handwriting
RO "Mia, Mia Veselia"
EN "Mia, Mia the Joy of Life"
From the author's personal collection

Excerpt (middle stanza) in English:

"Mia, Mia, the joy,
She inspires cheerfulness
In tired souls
Tormented by life."

Mia in Her Own Words

1994 (I)

Writing these lines comes with great difficulty. But it is only like this that one can understand why spring brings me so much joy, why in spring I am so happy to be alive. And in fall everything is sad for me, just as my life has been from the moment my father was arrested and until the moment I met my guardian angel, my husband Ciprian. In 1964, I was angry at God. Today, in 1994, as I am writing this, I feel grateful, and I am praying. I have made peace with the "cross" of my life. We each have our own cross to carry.

Flower Girl

"Where are you heading to, dear flower girl,
so early in the morning? I'm heading
to the beautiful field to pick up delicate flowers.
Pink roses, red poppies, come on, bloom!
Happy mood, you're everywhere,
today's the flowers' ball!"

Romanian children's song

1957

End of the school year. I remember my beautiful, long, and large pink dress; the high, pink, boron hat; the splendid rose bouquet. Their thorns pricked me, but I ignored them. Instead, I went on smiling happily to the audience in the room.

Later in life, I became somewhat of a flower girl. I gave love and friendhship until the world started, gradually, to no longer need such poor flowers.

The Doll

In the fall of 1957, when I was 10, in the depth of the financial crisis, I saw a doll in a shop window. My father bought it for me. Looking at the doll today, in 1994, I can still feel the joy I felt in that moment. The doll is 13 cm tall, she is wearing a blue veil on her head, a pink dress with laces that makes her look like a princess, and a string of beads around her neck.

The years have passed and many sad things have happened, but my father's good thoughts from the world beyond have always focused towards "his doll," me. With his help and the help of God and of my guardian angel, Ciprian, I gave birth to a "living doll", the little princess of our family: Diana. Today, when she looks at my doll, she can you tell many stories about her grandfather Iuliu and about her mother's doll, although she has never met her grandfather.

The Postcard

September 1962. The first time we had news from *tata* after his trial. Until now we had no clue where he was being held, if he was healthy, if he was still alive.

What *mama* had declared as formal reason for filing for divorce (which was what most wives of political prisoners had to do back then to protect their children) was that he had "left his home and family 2 years ago, his place of residence remains unknown." *Mama,* a religious woman and daughter of a priest. Until this letter came from Periprava, 2 years after they had taken him away, nobody in our family or circle of friends knew where he was. I came home from a day out with my high-school at the Botanical Gardens in the district of *Plopi* (Popplars), tired but happy about the plant biology lesson received in the heart of nature. And there it was, the postcard.

But the text, as we found out later, was not written by *tata,* but predefined and imposed to all prisoners – written by a military graduate with the chalk on the black board of the Periprava labor camp, where *tata* was *living,* as we found out that day, 2 years after his arrest.

20.IX.1962

My dears,

Find about me that I am well, which I wish to you too. I have the right to one food package containing 1 kg bacon, 4 kg sugar and 400 cigarettes *Mărăşeşti.* The food altogether should not weigh more than 5 kg. Also include 2 or 3 postcards. If you do not respect the above, the package will be returned.

Kisses,

Iuliu

Sender address:
IOANOVICI IULIU
Formatiunea M.A.I.
PERI – PRAVA – Grind
(raion Tulcea)

The Old Ways of Life
Technology

RO În 1957 nu existau nici casetofoane, nici tehnica video nu pătrunsese la noi. Erai fericită să te joci, să te plimbi cu trotineta, cu bicicleta, să-ţi confecţionezi singură păpuşi, să te joci cu pisicile, câinii (blocurile nu apăruseră şi ca atare viaţa multor copii se desfăşura în curte şi nu...în balcon, sau în faţa blocului...), să fii fericit că eşti copil şi să-ţi trăieşti clipele frumoase (ca de exemplu ziua numelui), să trăieşti liber şi fără prea multe formalităţi (deşi pe-atunci părinţii noştri o duceau destul de greu).

EN In 1957 there were no tape players and the video technology had not yet made it to Romania either. Back then, you were happy just to play, to ride your scooter or bike, to make your own dolls, to play with the cats, with the dogs (there were no tall flat buildings yet, only houses, and thus the life of many children would take place in the courtyard and not...on the balcony, or in front of the building...), to be happy to be a child and live your beautiful moments (like for instance your Name Day), to live freely and without too much formality (although back then our parents were living a rather rough life).

Summer Holidays

Lugoj

1960. Summer heat on the banks of the river Timiş. *Uica* Liviu (Uncle Liviu), *tata*'s cousin from Lugoj, invited me and my sister Dorina to spend 14 days of our summer holidays at his place. He lived close to the train station (where he was also working as *impiegat de mişcare* – EN "employee of movement") with his wife Leli and her parents (the Dobrescu family). Doctor Dobrescu was himself imprisoned, like *tata*. *Uica Liviu* was a great swimmer.

1970. *Uica Liviu* came to Timişoara to pick me up and took me to Oradea, where I had been placed to work after my university studies. He died of a bad heart, but before that he had told me the secret of life: "Mia, make sure you have a family of your own, including a child."

Sânnicolaul Mare

In June 1994, I receive a postcard from my cousin Olimpia. Her elder son Edi got a baby girl. I have so many fond memories of my cousins Olimpia and Tibi and their parents Madga and *Uica* Gheorghe, my father's brother, and their old house in *Sânnicolaul Mare*.

I remember Tibi (born 1 day apart from my husband Ciprian and thus 8 years my senior), a high-school student in Timişoara back then, dressing up as Santa Claus for me, and me pretending to still believe in Santa Claus to make him happy.

One summer, Dorina and I visited them during our school vacation, as always. The river Aranca was flowing at the edge of their garden. Tibi would invoke it:

RO *Doamne, dă să ploaie*
Să curgă șiroaie,
Să crească Aranca,
Să mă plimb cu barca.

EN God, let it rain,
Let it pour,
Let the Aranca rise
So I can sail on it.

One afternoon, Olimpia, the beautiful girl of the family, took my measures while I was sleeping and sew a summer dress for me. When I woke up, it was already waiting for me to try it on. Her big talent was also drawing, not just sewing. I also remember how in summer she would go down to their basement and prepare ice cream (back then not everyone had a fridge but everyone had a cool basement). One would get good cold water from the *arteză* by using *chițeanul* (words in Banatian dialect). Back then, *Uica* Gheorge was a primary school teacher and *Tanti* Magda was the best housewife, especially when it came to baking. We would all eat her cake with great pleasure.

Bogda

I remember being on summer camp at Bogda, while Dorina was studying for her high-school leaving exam. Not far from here, at Lipova, *tata* used to work as a notary when I was 2 years old. I slept in that building once. To this day, my heart gets sad when I see groups of children getting ready to leave to Bogda on summer camp and I remember those days.

Sculea

I remember going with Dorina to Sculea, for Christmas or summer vacation, to stay with *Finul* and *Fina* and their daughters, Dica and Cheți, before the big 15th of August (Virgin Mary) celebration. My maternal grandfather was a primary school teacher here. Together with *mama,* they were the godparents of Ana and Mihai Adam, a long time ago. Both Ana and Mihai Adam were good souls, sensitive, with a lot of common sense, like most Romanian peasants from the Banat region, who went through a lot of trouble both before and after collectivization. In their old house on the hill, next to the road, at Sculea, I learned to dance for the summer festivities and befriended Lili, the priest's daughter.

Dica and Dorina would sell watermelon, yelling from the depth of their lungs:

"Come buy watermelon, it is very tasty! Come get watermelon, we are selling it cheap!"

At the summer festivities, Dica and Cheți's mother *Fina* was a dedicated cook. She'd make:

- yellow soup with noodles
- *carne pane* or roasted bird meat (chicken, goose, or turkey)
- her famous *sarmale* (sour cabbage rolls filled with minced meat, onion, and rice)
- all sorts of cake.

There would also be beer and cold water, fresh from the fountain. The table would be full of specialties to welcome the guests.

Years later, Dorina would get married at the church in Sculea and I at the church in Gătaia (the priest was, of course, Lili's father). We both celebrated our weddings at the old house in Sculea.

Pîrvova

Pîrvova is a small village near Iablanița, in the Herculane area. I used to spend my childhood summers here before 1959, with my parents and my sister, visiting relatives of my maternal grandmother. On the way from Iablanița by bus, I would get carsick, and my mother would treat me with the anti-nausea lotion Diana.

Uica Matei and *Tușa* Sofia had a house with many rooms on the river shore. One of my favorite memories from here is the Annual Parade of Traditional Clothing. There would be traditional music and lots of stands selling gingerbread. The kids, including myself, would all rush to buy gingerbread.

Tata would write new poems and edit older ones. He always had a kind word for everyone.

We children would play outside all day, on the river banks, where women wearing traditional clothing would do their families' laundry with *maiul*, against the rocks. Then we would go to the *colibă* to eat hot, freshly cooked *coleșă* (*RO mămăligă*, EN "polenta"), usually with fried cheese. Evenings, we would bring the cows home and milk them. *Uica* Matei and *Tușa* Sofia would work on the field all day, while my grandmother would cook for all of us. I remember collecting hay into haystacks and the scarecrows that would make us children laugh. Evenings I would nest into my father's arms and tell him everything about my day's adventures. I once attended a funeral in Pîrvova. The cemetery of Pîrvova was far away, up on a tall hill, and from the house of the deceased to the cemetery, *bocitoarele* (EN "the howlers") would howl painfully, as if the world were about to end, all the way up to the top of the hill.

To this day, Pîrvova remains a place of a happy childhood for me, a memory sprinkled with the white flowers of the beautiful days, dear days, full-of-memories-about-*tata* days.

I have not made it back to Pîrvova since he died.

High-School Graduation
July 1965. I graduated from Școala Medie Nr. 5, on Strada Simion Bărnuțiu Nr. 5. We were 9 girls and 23 boys in the science section (Maths, Physics, and Chemistry). The school leaving party took place at the Military Casino, after we passed our exams:

- Romanian and Maths: written and oral exams
- oral exams only: Physics, Chemistry, History, and Socialism.

Manual Labor

I remember spring cleaning at our house. Everything had to be washed, ironed, folded. I didn't like doing any of that. I wanted to read, walk towards *Pădurea Verde* (EN "The Green Forest"), go to shows: film, theater, opera, or music concerts. Some members of my family wanted me to become a seamstress. My grandmother was against it and saved me. I ended up studying industrial chemistry but didn't enjoy it. Now, at 47 years old, I'm doing a different kind of labor: writing. Asking my husband to check what I wrote and whether it's any good.

The Mill

Sunday mornings, Diana-*Țuchi* and I go to the cemetery where *tata* is buried. Then we go to my mother's place for lunch. After lunch, we all 3 play *Moara* (EN "The Mill"). I remember how in my childhood, in the 50s, we would play it with buttons or white beans. We did not have plastic pieces back then like today. We sometimes play *Moara* for 3 hours straight.

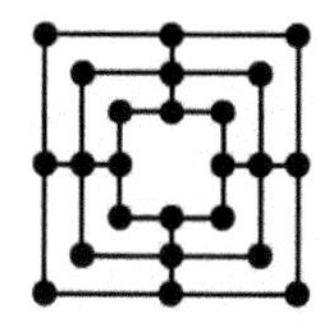

As a child, I used to play it with my parents. My father knew a lot of tricks. I tell Diana many stories about him, with the hope that nothing about his life, character, and doings will ever be forgotten, that we will always keep him among us, in our souls, as a living presence to guide our steps further with his unique insight.

1994 (II)

The acacia tree in front of our house is blooming. Each time it rains, I look at it and remember my father. I remember how my father would take me out for a walk to *Pădurea Verde*, back when we had another acacia tree in front of another house...back when I still had a road to follow and a guardian angel.

The strong pillar of our family, my father, died 30 years ago, a ridiculous death. The strong tree of my childhood, my father, my mother, my sister, was strongly chopped, butchered.

My father's absence deeply marked all 3 of us (my mother, my sister, and me) and pushed us into chaos. While my father *lived* behind bars, we were...free (as a manner of speaking...), for there was no such thing as freedom; families of political prisoners were under constant surveillance.

Such families had to be brought to exasperation at any cost and through any means: the daughters were to either marry "sweet" informers or, alternatively, to be publicly shamed and declared one or more of the following: informers, prostitutes, crazy, plus they would have to be professionally persecuted through all possible means. Such women were supposed to work with their hands, not with their heads.

Thus, I still feel the bars of my so-called freedom even today, in 1994. The years of poverty, humiliation, fear, the strong lack of money, the inferiority complexes towards the rest of the world will never be erased.

Towards which branches will life carry us?

Mia through Diana's Eyes

Twelve (II)

1959. My mother is 12 and she is not my mother yet. She is a sister and a daughter, but also herself. A child who likes to play outside and read books more than anything else.

I imagine her coming home from school one afternoon and seeing their house damaged, clothes everywhere, as if someone had been impatiently looking for something or someone they couldn't immediately find. And then the understanding: my grandfather, her father, gone. And my grandmother, the one who has to break down the news to her daughters: their father has been arrested.

At his mock-trial in 1960, my child-mother runs to hug her father before he's taken back behind bars. She whispers into his ear: "Don't worry about us, *Ticule*. We will be fine." They won't. I imagine her elder sister, my aunt, only 19 years old, looking at the university admission boards, her name removed, tears gathering in her eyes, her legs trembling, then running without her, up to the edge of the town. She wouldn't return home until dark. "Dirty political background" is what she'll keep hearing from now on. What they'll keep hearing about themselves, over and over again, when doors will get slammed into their faces for no good reason.

I imagine my grandmother filing for divorce to improve my mother's high-school application folder, taking a job, her first ever, as an unqualified worker, in the invalid section at the accordion factory to make ends meet for her and her girls, and even that only thanks to family friends who dare use their connections and defy the oppressive political system of their times.

I imagine my grandfather released from prison, in 1962, earlier than planned, sent back home, to his ex-wife and daughters. Unemployed for a full 6 months. Then eventually working again but at DCA, as a planner in the waste factory, no longer allowed to profess his job as a notary. A living corpse. Sent home to die.

I imagine my mother holding her father's hand in hospital, in 1963, his arm swollen and blue from too many blood transfusions that change nothing.

I imagine my mother in 1964, only 16 years old, kissing her father on his lips, when his eyes close for the last time. A promise that he can no longer hear: "Our souls will always, always be together." She holds his death certificate in her hand and through her tears she still sees the fake diagnosis: pneumonia, instead of leukemia. They even turned his death into a lie.

At his funeral, she wears a plain black cotton dress, with a tight ribbon around the neck. Her grandmother stands next to her, holding 2 long candles crossed in a handkerchief in her left hand. My mother kisses my grandfather's dead face and covers it in tears. The undertakers pull her away, but her eyes keep following the coffin. They are covering the coffin. They are pounding long black nails, 8 in total, into the coffin. They are lowering it down, into the deep dark wet ground, and covering it with freshly dug soil. It is starting to rain. Poor children gather to get *colivă*.

My mother plays these scenes in her head over and over again, searching for meaning, but there is no meaning, only more loss and confusion. And she never ever talks about these things out loud, "because walls have ears."

I don't imagine these things chronologically, as they happened. I imagine them because my mother, before collapsing into a long-lasting depression, wrote them down.

1994. She is 47 when it happens. I am 12. A child who likes to play outside and read books more than anything else.

My Mother Sells Water from the Fountain

My mother sells water from the fountain, 20 *bani* a cup.

There's a heat wave in this city,
There's thirst and hunger in this country.
On some days, the hunger can still be fought.

There are things in this city, in this country,
Things not to be talked about,
Family members held silent behind bars.

Books my child-mother reads on her birthday with her friend S.,
whose father is also not to be talked about.
Dissidents! Criminals! Traitors of their country!

The cherry flowers are in full bloom,
There is still unpoisoned water in the fountain
And books to be passed around.

My mother sells water from the fountain, 20 *bani* a cup.

The Blue Fish

When my parents get engaged in 1980, my father doesn't give my mother a ring, but a necklace. The necklace has a fish attached to it, the color of water, or of the clear sky. *Albastru ceruleum* (EN "Cerulean blue"). The mouth of the fish is orange and wide open. The chain itself is of silver, but not the kind most people wear. It has many links. One day it breaks, one link of the chain lets go of the next. I keep it when my mother stops wearing it, even though it is broken and never again gets fixed.

Wedding Picture

It is April 1980. The spring flowers are in bloom in her hands. There's a shadow on the wooden fence and on the door that stands closed behind them, but not a cloud in the sky. Her ankles are thin; one leg is slightly bent. His hand is resting on her shoulder, his fingers thick, swollen, red. It's not the first time that he's doing the marriage thing, but he is smiling. She is not. She cannot pose for the camera. She will never learn. The garden where they are standing is her mother's, but they will not live here. The story will unfold itself, her womb will live and die, there will and won't be children. But right now, it is spring. The red brick road unfolds in front of them. Their hands will still find each other even 30, even 40 years from now, even in more than one hospital bed, even in the darkness that she cannot escape. Perhaps he will rescue her. Perhaps she will rescue herself.

Family Story

When I'm 2 years old, we move from a small flat to a big flat with tall walls in a tall, old house. When cars pass on the street, the whole house shakes. But now this is our home. Or at least it should be. In the first weeks, the walls are so tall that I cry at night when my parents let me sleep alone. I cry instead of sleeping. There is too much space around me that is not filled by my mother. That is not my mother. I can only fall asleep if my mother is next to me, if she wraps her arms tightly around me. The walls are tall and I long for walls that are closing in on me. This is my parents' interpretation, at least. It becomes one of our core family stories.

My Feet Don't Even Touch the Ground

When I am 5, at Lake Secu, or later, when I am 7, at Lake Mărghitaș, my mother carries me on her frontside; in her arms I am safe, and my legs and feet don't hurt from walking. When she carries me, they don't even touch the ground. When I am 6, at Lake Mărghitaș, my parents and I wander over the hills and my father takes photos of everything. My mother carries me in her arms or on her back. Sometimes I walk by myself, but she is always there, next to me, to give me a hug, guide my steps, or hold my hand. She's always there. Even when the rats eat biscuits on my father's chest at night, she and I are together and sleep through it all, undisturbed by the noise they make with their tiny little teeth and feet. Undisturbed by the diseases they might carry.

Mirror (I)

I am 5. I call my father *my brother, Paul,* although his real name is *Cipri*. I call my mother *mama*. They call me nicknames: *Țuchi, Tontel,* or *Pisicii Tăi*. I don't like any of these names.

My mother takes care of me, but with my father, I laugh, do yoga, paint. On New Year's Day, he and I paint the door of his art studio together. We paint the numbers that make the year we're entering, spirals, flowers, and stars.

It is my father who makes up stories for me at night, when I cannot fall asleep. Once I am asleep, my father goes to his bed, and my mother comes next to me for the night. My mother does not tell me made up stories, she only tells me real stories about her father, my grandfather. Whenever I ask her to tell me or make up a story for me, afternoons, when she gets home tired from work, she falls asleep right after "Once upon a time, there was a little girl...*A fost odată ca niciodată, a fost odată o fetiță...*" I cannot sleep, so I wake her up to continue, but she's too tired. So I just lay awake beside her and when she wakes up we go to the nearby park. To play. But she doesn't let me do much. She's always afraid that I'll fall and break an arm or leg. Her arms are almost always around me.

But once she is not careful and in *Mica*'s garden I try to leap over the whole flight of stairs and I land on my arm and head. I do not break my arm and I do not crack my head as so many children in *Kindergarten* often do. There is no blood, just the shock of hitting the hard surface. She is angry and yelling. At me but mostly at herself, I think.

I often get punished for taking risks and craving more independence. Like that one time at Gărâna when I am 10 and take off over the hills without telling her, knowing my father is painting just a couple of hills further away. I take off and keep walking to find him. She realizes where I might be heading, comes after me, and drags me back through the moory summer land. Then, in the evening, she tells everyone at the art summer camp what I did. I feel ashamed, which is what she aims for so that I learn my lesson and never do it again.

In Timișoara, my father never joins us at the big *Parcul Copiiilor* (EN "the Children's Park"). It's just my mother and me. Every time we come here, I want us to go to the Train of Horrors and the Mirrors' Room. She does not look at our reflections. "They deform us," she says. But I like these funny shapes: we are square, or round, or even not like ourselves at all, so I make it a habit to look at the 2 of us for her too. In some mirrors, we blend.

Here, she looks nothing like the portrait my father painted of her, the one in my room. There, she has long curly red hair. Like fire, but in a good way.

"I love you," she says, and I believe it.

I believe her.

I believe everything she says.

City Walks

My mother and I take long walks along the *Bega* river, which flows through our city and is the first river to be turned into a channel in our country. Forced to go from wild and random to contained and disciplined. Apparently, that kind of river is a good thing to have in a city. There are many willows along the river's shore. *Salcii plângătoare* (EN "Weeping willows"). At least this is what she tells me. Their branches and leaves face the surface of the earth and of the water, and sometimes they get into the water, or at least touch its surface. They do not face the sky like other trees. That is what makes willows so special, my mother tells me. I love willows and later other trees, too. When we start learning plant biology in school, flowers and trees are all I talk about.

My Mother Gets Fired

1994. She comes home and does not say anything. Her employer fires her because she challenged her performance evaluation. They send her off to the psychiatric hospital, but she doesn't go. She does not tell us anything about it. Instead, she plays the music too loud. She pretends to go to work for a few days afterwards but then she gives up and just stays at home. She keeps telling people that she is pregnant but it turns out to be just a fibroid in her uterus, one she will never have removed; her whole uterus is *fibrous*. Being fired triggers what is seen as psychosis – she is convinced she is being persecuted due to her family's past, convinced she is followed by Securitate, and perhaps she is. A few weeks later she gets another diagnosis: bipolar disorder. She enters early retirement on the grounds of illness and will never return to work, neither here nor elsewhere. On the background of the raging hormonal changes and the overall mess, trying to write about her father breaks her. The world around her is spinning and she is spinning with it. We are spinning with her. I am only 12. My world turns dark.

Silence(d) (I)

mother was swallowed by sharks –
she had bent down to pick up seashells for me,
on the river shore:
first her hair,
then her eyes,
then her mouth.
now all mother's words
are being carried on water,
while mother is silent,
like a fish.

My Mother Is Sleeping

My mother and I share a bed until she turns into someone else.
When she stops bathing and her smell changes,
When all that's left of her is constant pain,
She turns into someone else.
On some mornings, she wakes up early,
Then falls, next to the bed.
I pick her up.
And then I don't want to sleep with her anymore.

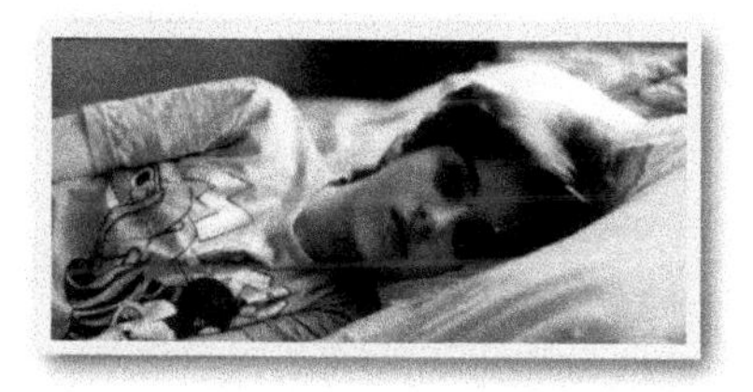

Where Is My Mother?

my mother dissolves.
no, she evaporates.
no, I am making this up.

this isn't my mother!
this woman
who doesn't eat,
doesn't bathe,
doesn't go to work anymore.

who is she?
she is a stranger
with no arms left
to hold my own.

The Daughter Becomes Mother

Then it all changes again. She spends most days in bed. She doesn't eat. She doesn't cry. She doesn't smile. Menopause. Manic-depressive disorder. Depression. She's 47. Nothing makes sense. "I love you," she says, "but I can no longer prove it." The drugs make her sleep most of the time. Sometimes she says she wants to die. Her hands tremble. She hallucinates. Side effects. I cry all the tears that she cannot cry. I make up stories in order to survive. Sometimes, I believe them. But I even fail at that: I only manage to believe some of them, not all. Some stories are better left unwritten, undreamed, untold. And then, to dream, I write poetry instead.

Willow

The willow danced, her moves did not care about the crowd, her hands drew circles in the air, like caterpillars falling down from apples, they crossed over unseen faces, caressing their every pore, she twirled embracing human bodies only she could see, and the room was dark, and still, and the light was red, in the theater-podium bar, and only the little black cat in the corner watched and whispered through her purrs to the trees in the forest in which she thought she was, she said, look, although there is no river, and no human to cry next to her, here's a willow with a female face, with long dark-red hair that falls onto stones like branches, a woman who forgot to dream but became a dream herself, forsaken by male touch and baby hugs, look, the cat said, there's a woman almost taking off and leaving the ground, rooting her hands deep into the clouds, but the cat was just a cat, and the forest did not listen, because there was no forest, and there was no ground, and the music stopped, and the willow was now asleep, with a little black blind kitten curled up at her feet, and the next performance, and the audience, they were nowhere to be found, and the willow's voice was dreaming of a time when she used to sing each night, it was either opera or jazz, and the willow was young and voluptuous back then, she was nothing like a willow at all, and the willow's voice fell asleep too, deep in her stomach, away from human sounds, behind the curtains, and never again was it to be found.

Silence(d) (II)

When you live with someone with chronic suicidal depression, your own, regular sadness gets unnoticed, even if you are a child. It is too banale, too ordinary. There's no room and time for it. It becomes impractical to even feel it, year after year after year. Always there.

The Cage (I)

With my mother's spirit gone, I look for other reference points, but cannot find them. My overwhelmed father keeps telling me: "You are young, you must endure. You must stay strong." My mother's unbearable sadness spreads over our house like a tent. Inside the tent, there isn't room for anyone else's sadness except her own. But the tent has holes in it and the rain still gets in.

Who is this woman? My mother used to be the center of my world. And now she has totally lost her own center.

I learn to patch my own wounds, apply my own makeup. I make a lot of mistakes that nobody knows anything about. I learn to pretend that everything's alright. Sometimes I even believe it. If I feel sad, for instance, or scared, or restless, I shove it all down, into the places of myself that resemble my mother, the places I never look at for too long.

I am not like my mother, I am like my father, I keep telling myself. My father becomes my anchor. There is no other way.

I train myself to be funny, to laugh, to entertain people, including myself. I get so good at it that nobody suspects a thing about my family, about my mother. I simply tell my friends that she is not pregnant (all the ones she got to brag to about it) when asked, then change the topic fast. And I do not speak about her not working anymore. Everything is just fine, I say.

When she speaks, my mother who refuses to eat keeps warning us that there isn't enough food in the fridge. That we need to buy more. We tell her we have enough but she keeps saying the same things, on repeat.

"Who is cooking for you?" she asks. Sometimes my aunt or grandmother. Sometimes my father. "But I don't always need warm food," I tell her, "I can get by."

"Who is taking care of our house? I can't do a thing," she says. "I have no strength to take care of it, to clean it, to tidy up. Do you remember how I used to be?"

Who is this woman, who cannot eat, who cannot sleep, who smells like a stranger?

"Don't worry," I tell her, but the chaos outside and inside of myself keeps getting larger.

I am 15 when my father has severe internal bleeding from his ulcerus and is taken to the hospital in an ambulance. His last words before going out the door that evening are: "We may not see each other again, take care of your mother." But he returns, and for a long time all he can eat is bananas and vegetable soup at room temperature, but then my grandmother dies, just a few days later. My mother, who has been doing a little better than usual for the last couple of months (like eating without being pushed to do it), has another relapse. She sleeps through her mother's funeral, and, 4 years later, through her sister's. My mother keeps on spending most of her life in bed, not always quite falling asleep.

I am a trapped animal who cannot choose which way to go, or whether to leave the cage. I am a half-grown disoriented pup and my mother is here with me in the cage. She is and she isn't. My father seals the cage in gold. "This is our home," he says. "This is where we belong." But I do not believe him. I do not belong here. I belong on fields and streets that are not in this city, this country. Somewhere where nobody knows me but where I do not have to seek love because I can easily find it. I belong in mountains and valleys and on the lips of strangers. But I am only a child and I cannot choose. My father won't even let me go out for walks. Who is she? Who am I? Why are we hanging on instead of letting go?

Each day the same, we wake up and pretend like nothing has happened. Like everything is fine. And we do not talk about it out loud. Not out in the open. I start to bleed before she stops bleeding. The cage is not large enough to hold us both. All I can do is yell and scream. It changes nothing. The plot is the same every day, for the rest of our lives.

She is shrinking from not eating but the cage is still not large enough to hold us both. Day after day, week after week, month after month, year after year.

I write poetry.

In the mirror I sometimes look like her. But my hunger to be out in the world and do my own thing is so much bigger. I get out of the cage at times but I always return.

I never leave. My father comes back from hospital and I am there. He is there. My mother is there. The pain is always here and it stinks.

The cage no longer pretends to be golden, it is just a cage. Never let go, never let go. Hold on, hold on. It is our duty, it is our duty.

There is no privacy inside the cage. When the phone rings, everyone listens and interferes with the ongoing conversation.

"We love you very much."

"I love you," she says, "but I cannot show it to you. You do not understand what is happening inside my head. I have no words to tell you how entangled everything is."

Her words seem void of meaning. She keeps saying them, over and over again. I yell, I scream. I blame her for abandoning me, for no longer playing her mother role. "Making a daugher is not enough, you cannot give up, it is your duty to also raise her!"

I accuse her of giving up on our family. I yell at her a lot. All the time. A lot. She turns her back to me and sleeps. Like my anger and tears make no difference. My pain will not bring her back, so what is the point of feeling it?

I go to the movies but I always return. Day after day, week after week, month after month, year after year. I almost have her hair. I do not have her cheekbones.

I am only 15 and I haven't even kissed a boy yet. At the Black Sea that summer, I am the only one in the group not wearing makeup. No, not that summer. Who am I, who will I become? I do not know. I take many walks on my own, along the sea shore. A man shows up from behind a rock. He is not wearing any pants.

"Do you want me to lick your cunt?"

"No! Let go," I scream and hit him, with my purse, his penis errect in his hands.

"Let go!", I scream and hit him harder. I run but he is not chasing me.

"You dropped your sunscreen," he yells from behind.

I go back to pick it up. Then I run some more.

It is my first time at the sea and a warning, to never walk alone. When I feel like it is safe to do so, I stop at the shore, just near the water, and for a long time, all I do is just sit on the sand, watch the waves, and tremble. It feels like the trembling will never leave me.

I return to the city. I go back to my cage that no longer pretends to be of gold. I always, always go back. And I never, never let go. I am told all the time not to let go.

"Get used to things never improving," her friend tells me one day. But I can't do that. In parallel, I plot my escape.

I Imagine

I imagine my mother as a child, sitting at a desk, reading the books that I will later discover in our home library, all the books that the censors had failed to ban. I imagine her, my aunt, my grandmother, sitting around the kitchen table, at the dim light of the oil lamp, during electricity cuts. I imagine their extended family both helping them and pulling away. I imagine the loneliness of losing a parent at the age of 12. I can feel it too.

What I do not know yet:
Families have scripts that they repeat and pass on,
until someone comes along and breaks the chain.

I imagine the hopelessness, like a snake grappling at your throat, making your heart race, without escape, hour after hour, day after day, living in "freedom", outside the bars. I imagine the poverty, the hunger. How it all gets normalized after a while. I imagine my mother reading the postcard that my grandfather writes from prison, but it is a standardized text, these are not his words; "he" is asking for the family to send him bacon, sugar, and cigarettes (although he himself never smoked). The amounts are very specific. It is what we get when I am a child too with our monthly ration. And it is "normal" not to have more. I imagine my mother, at the end of high-school, not long after watching her father sink into the ground, choosing to study Chemistry over Literature. Later, I repeat her choice. And, like her, I regret it, too.

What I do not know yet:
Families have scripts that they repeat and pass on,
until someone comes along and breaks the chain.

I imagine her learning to conform, bend her head, neither have nor express any opinions of her own, especially not in front of men. I imagine her voice, the one that would sing and laugh, buried deep inside her, without sound. My mother, the no-longer-weeping-and-mostly-sleeping willow. I do not want to think of myself as her. Even her name, Maria, means bitterness. It is hard to believe that she was once her father's *Mia, Mia, veselia.*

Voice III – Diana

(Words in the World)

Where Are You From?

The Suitcase

My luggage, when I move to Bremen, Germany in early October 2004, contains:

- warm clothes for the winter, including an extra thick, knee-long black jacket that definitely makes me look fat but serves its purpose
- my 10 most beloved books in Romanian
- a sleeping bag for the first night at the hostel near the train station; I have no flat for the nights after
- the Marla Singer space monkey boots, as I call them
- a black velvet blazer from a second hand store
- hippie dresses from *Piața Flavia* that will no longer fit me in less than a year
- old rings and earrings from *Piața Flavia*
- hair spinning scissors
- a lot of fear and a lot of expectations
- low self-worth mixed with high ambitions
- probably too many socks (especially warm ones, for the winter) and too much underwear
- small gin bottles from *Metro*
- *Kit Kat* - lots of them
- many sandwiches (I have lost count)
- car sickness medicine (*Emetiral*)

- passport with visa (my visa is valid for 9 months)
- Euro coins to use the bathrooms on the highways, when crossing borders
- liters of water for the 30-hour long bus ride
- old cell phone with Romanian SIM card
- a home-sewed little sack with 1,000 Euro cash hanging from a thick thread around my neck, underneath my blouse
- envelopes with more cash placed in different parts and pieces of my luggage, so that, if one envelope gets stolen, I will still have money left.

Later, after several crossings of borders with many hours of waiting, at the hostel, after 30 hours on the bus, I wrap the sleeping bag around me completely although I feel too hot, with my little cash bag still tied around my neck, so that nobody will dare steal from me. I only sleep for 4-5 hours because I need to be at the International Office at 8:30 am, somewhere near a glass building on campus; I manage to get a student dorm room, all to myself, with help from the International Office. Someone cancelled last minute, so I got her place. It is only 20 m^2 but it fits my budget.

I need help to move my luggage from the hostel basement because I packed too many things. I speak broken German and get asked a lot:

"Can you please speak English instead?"

When my grandfather was sent to prison against his will, did they let him pack anything?

—∾—

You touch money and walls for days that turn into months
into years,
There are old tall buildings in the gray city, meant to make
people fear God,

Not just now, but since the dark and not forgotten Middle Ages.
They speak of things other than yourself and your memories.
You listen to the old *pianină* singing tunes that sound the same
Each Friday afternoon and you do not feel any loving presence.
You touch money and you do not dare convert them anymore,
From them you could buy houses instead of bread in another
country.
You buy more bread and stop counting
The money, the days, all the times you did not touch another
human.

Although I live in Germany in 2005, life in Romania goes on, like a parallel movie in a "what if" scenario, except that I cannot fully escape it and I am part of 2 scenarios at once – one that I tried to leave behind and another one that I cannot claim as my own.

Just before Christmas, when I visit my parents for what other families know as "good old family time" and actually look forward to, my mother is convinced that she has been saved by Jesus and stops taking her medication. It is her second maniacal phase since the official start of her illness in 1994. She spends a lot of money, buys a lot of things, goes to church every day, and almost never sleeps. She is writing about her father again, pages and pages of handwritten notes, with many details about how she is being followed. It is a horrible Christmas, but then again, most Christmases have been horrible in the last 10 years, full of "I want to die, life has no meaning. One day I will turn on the gas in our kitchen and then I will be truly gone." Through most of the year, I would be able to distract myself outside of our home and try to live an almost normal life. But holidays, Christmas, Easter, were harder to face. All my friends were with their families and I had no choice but to be with mine. Everything was closed. I had nowhere to go.

"The doll is cursed," Mother says.
She throws it away.
The doll goes away, but the stories stay.
We are the living dolls now.
But the story, our main story — is gone.
The doll comes back and stays in my room.

I leave my parents again in January 2006, in the heart of winter, once again the whole journey by bus, back to my *life* in Bremen, where my almost boyfriend dumps me without actually informing me of it (he made up with his ex-girlfriend in Romania over the holidays, as I find out after confronting him several times).

In parallel, my mother's mania unravels further, she develops what is clinically known as "affective inversion" towards my father, who ends up calling an ambulance; a nurse injects sleeping medication against my mother's will and my father starts putting medication into my mother's food without her knowledge.

A few months later, her mood stabilizes, she is neither depressed nor maniacal and operates almost like a "normal" being. My parents start having a social life again. I am not there.

When I am there, my mother tells me: "Please don't get angry at me for saying this, I am not saying it to hurt you, but I am not used to having you around anymore."

I am not there in my own body in Bremen, my calcium drops frequently, I have panic attacks, I have no reference points, I have never before felt so lost and lonely. I relive the things I left behind and want to talk about them, but there's nobody to listen. The almost boyfriend always blocked personal conversations by saying things like: "Don't tell me, I don't want to know."

—

I thought life abroad would mean I would get to make my own decisions, have opportunities, go on adventures. But I cannot even go out with the other Erasmus students because one drink (even a small bottle of Coca-Cola, 200 mL, not 250 mL like in Romania) costs 2.5 Euro. I do not even dare convert the expenses here into tens of thousands of *lei*, and less after the *Leu* becomes RON. It takes me years, even after I start earning money during my PhD (although I am paid poorly compared to the hours I spend working in the lab, at night and on weekends too), to feel comfortable paying for a meal in a restaurant, I keep obsessing over how many poor families could make a living for weeks in Romania with the money my new friends and I spend in one night.

The guilt almost never leaves me.

—

On the Way

city of my childhood,
you're like a forgotten body
I can no longer own.
I remain a passenger through you,
who can never return.

2011

You are in Banff National Park, Canada. It is a day in summer, a day like any other. It is your last day here. Summer is coming to an end. Tomorrow your visa will expire. Today you are here, tomorrow you will be gone. Everything has been packed. Your identity too. Your personality is ready for something new, or something along those lines. Maybe this is the last time ever that you see the Rockies from such a close distance, that you can breathe them in, feel them with your whole body, discover them, take them inside you. Soon you'll turn 29, and soon after that 30. You are traveling light. After so many years of inner and outer abroad-ness, you have finally learned how to pack. You gave away the books, almost all of them. It hurt. There are also other things that hurt. There are people that you may never see again. Sulphur Mountain remains your magic mountain. Life will bring: bureaucratic chaos, moving, uncertainty.

Your taxi is here. The taxi driver asks, as he hears your accent in English: "Where is home?" You answer: "No clue." You breathe in silence and watch the motion of the trees, of the river, of the sun. You have learned to stop recounting your life story to every stranger, to stop selling your private life as small-talk topic, to stop summarizing it in a nice, cute, and digestible way. Through the open windows, you breathe in. And out.

You hand him the money. You tip generously. He wishes you all the best. Then you leave.

Today is your birthday. Or maybe tomorrow, or yesterday? It depends on where the time is currently being measured. In any case: today, yesterday, or tomorrow you are alone.

Early morning in the airport, on your birthday.

Morning here, evening there.

In Canada, England, Germany, Romania.

In an airport, you must always demonstrate your value. The untouchability of the human dignity – as the German constitution puts it – are empty words today. They anyhow apply to Germans only.

Birthday after birthday, we get closer to our death. *Death* is a feminine noun in your mother tongue. *Moarte. Death* will never be masculine to you, like it is in German. The same as *table, house,* and *boat. Sadness* remains feminine in both your mother tongue and German. *Traurigkeit. Tristeţe.*

2009

You wanted to study, you wanted to get away, you wanted to discover the whole world.

In the beginning, you were afraid of speaking German and of spending too much money. You ate a lot of bread and potato-salad. You gained weight. Your hair and fingernails became brittle. Your knee joints too. Your thyroid gland could not handle it any longer. You cannot imagine living like that nowadays, eating only bread. Bread, bread, bread. There are many types of bread in Germany, but none of them is the one you grew up with.

When you went away for the first time, you did not realize how hard it would be to one day come back, to truly return, even for just a short while. You could only move forward. After your first 9 months in Germany, you visited them. Your parents, your old friends. You could hardly believe that your old room was still there, on the same street, in the city where you spent the first 22 years of your life. Life in the never-really-forgotten place went on without you. Your best friend did not recognize your voice on the telephone.

Your old friends were now strangers. You wanted your old ego back, but it was not possible. Your eyes were open. And not just full of light, but also of darkness. The darkness of being alone on a Saturday night, the darkness of physical pain without a proper health insurance, the darkness of waiting in a hospital on a Sunday afternoon, for hours, and not being able to tell the doctor what hurts, and of asking stupid questions in front of the X-ray such as "What does it mean, *schwanger?*" The doctor explains to you how it works, the pregnancy thing. Your boyfriend (or something along those lines) can't help; he speaks even less German than you.

Here, abroad, when your parents come visit, you become the mother, and they the children. They do not want to leave the house without you. You cook for them every day. And they ask you many questions, about everything. You want them to never grow old and helpless. The abroad-ness makes everything worse.

The woman in your singing class is convinced that you work for either Amazon or McDonalds, like all Romanians. She is nothing but pure shock when she hears that you are a scientist with a PhD and fluent in 5 languages. She is a hairdresser. She only eats *bio*. In your home country, you did not have to question the *bio*-ness of the food, whether the hens were running free or not, whether today there was a market in town and where. Even today, your home town is full of open-air markets where peasants sell fresh products all day, every day. During the break, the woman does not ask you to join in for lunch with all the other classmates.

You always have to explain so much when you talk about your home country. What was it like to grow up in communism? Are you planning to ever move back? Most often you get asked when exactly is it that you will move back. And is life in your country really that bad and the corruption as big as the German newspapers say? Do you have any other family members in Germany? And why do you always talk in English at work? Why did you study in English in Germany and why did you stay here for so long? Why are you here?! Why won't you leave? Why are you still here? Justify your existence or leave!

Your childhood memories, your grandma's garden, where you would spend hours daydreaming and playing, where you would read books and eat cherries all summer, the hiking trips with your parents in the Carpathians, your father's art and chemistry-professorship, the joy you have always felt, even as a little girl, when it came to world history, culture, and literature, these are all topics that nobody wants to hear about. You come from Eastern Europe and everyone assumes that you speak Russian (you don't), and they laugh, and they ask you if you are a vampire, like Vlad Dracula. About gypsies you don't have to say anything, only the TV speaks about them; on TV they are always portrayed stealing but called Roma. Whoever happens to watch TV knows that actually all Romanians and Bulgarians are Roma, and the other way around. The newspapers also try to help you define your new identity and expand your vocabulary: parallel-society, poverty-based-immigration, qualified workers.

Each time you moved, you forgot a little more, a little faster, the meaning of the word *acasă*. You cannot really go back. You are no longer *tu*. You are envious, so incredibly envious, of all those people who have not lost their concept of home. All those people who are a lot younger than you are and already have 1 or 2 children and a house. Who have a good grasp of the language of the country they live in, regardless which country. Who do not think and speak in 3 languages even in their sleep. And you, what do you have? You have nothing. Nothing other than yourself. And you are not the person you thought you were. You are not the strong career woman with lots of interests that the others see in you.

You wanted to go see the world. But the world has seen enough Eastern-Europeans. Most people think that your mother tongue is Russian, or you know, one of those other slavic languages. And when they look at you, this is often all they see: an Eastern-European. On the train from Bremen to Norddeich Mole, deep in the North, a couple asked the 2 of you: "What kind of language is this, it sounds like Italian with a Russian accent?" "Romanian," you and the man next to you simultaneously said. They laughed. And you enwrapped yourselves in silence, but it wasn't the same silence. The man, the (boy)friend, although born in the same country as you, remained a stranger, even later, when he moved his body slowly and then faster and without words or emotions inside yours.

You make lists of how you feel: damaged, lost, forever. And also: lonely.

Now you feel abroad everywhere.

—~—

You move again. You are in an airport, destination: Canada.
The woman at the entrance wants to know
where you come from.
"That's a rather long story,"

you say.
She says:
"Your life doesn't interest me at all,
just show me your papers."
You cannot prove to her
that you come from a good country.
You may still be in this other place
and even remain here,
as long as you promise to leave
when you are no longer useful.
Your visa says: *Worker.*
You are a scientist with a PhD, therefore:
Worker – Biology.
Your heart says:
Whatever – but not really.
When you exit,
a man is waiting for you,
your man,
or something along those lines.

2010

And then it happens. Your man leaves you, you are sick, you have no job, you are either pregnant or carry a monster inside your belly, the monster must be taken out, but first they need to find the monster, nobody believes you when you talk about the monster, the monster is a part of you, you carry it around across countries, move after move, without knowing, the monster is you, you are the monster, somebody breaks into your new flat, you cannot sleep, you damage your knee, this time for good, what is wrong with you, you can't even walk, your boss wants to know why you are always sick, it is cold and dark in the lab, and outside even colder and darker, you are alone, all alone, you want to die, you cannot take it anymore, always alone, always unbelonging and lonely, you cannot go to a specialist, you have no car, it is -30 degrees Celsius outside, the mountains are beautiful, but you cannot walk, and anyway, this is not your home, what are you doing with your life, you stupid ugly slut, this is surely not your home, you lie down in the middle of the night in the middle of the street and tell your ex-man: I want to die, I cannot go on like this, he pulls you inside, you are in this-your flat, you and this estranged exotic man without a land, the man for whom you were not good enough, there is already another woman, she was your only friend here, this is so incredibly ordinary, he says: you need to come to terms with the new arrangements, please act like a grown-up, he says, please stop acting like this, you were so strong and independent when I first met you, he says, maybe this is the last time that we hug each other, he says, I cannot handle you in this helpless and emotional state, I cannot take this anymore, before that, earlier, he always said: you are the only family I ever had. It has been long, weeks, or months, or years, since he last spoke with his family. You only say: I want to die. And it just won't happen.

From your own fall
you need to learn
to breathe, to walk,
to define a new identity;
here, there, regardless where,
between colorful panels
and transit rooms.
Biology – Worker.

—w—

You begin to write. You attend a writing class each Tuesday. You call yourself writer. Your teacher talks about freefall-writing. Freefalling. You like the sound of it. You have always tried to be what you thought was expected of you. But at some point along the way it all fell apart. You are on the floor, in tiny little pieces, and you are no longer good enough, for anybody. The worst part is that you no longer know what to wish for, but you go on living.

> From your own sadness
> and unbelonging
> you build yourself a brand new *I*,
> without ever truly knowing
> the rules of the game.
> You make them up
> on the way,
> only for you and you alone,
> while you freefall,
> while you transform.
> A new home
> is slowly growing inside you.
> You become
> your *zuhause, acasă, home,*
> and everything in between.
> Everything else
> can be nothing else
> but nothing.
> You can only truly travel
> inside, on, and under you,
> with you.

2014

You are on vacation, in Norway. You are visiting a local museum. It's all about what it means to be Norwegian, and the old ways of life.

It is a day in summer, a day like any other. Summer is coming to an end. The receptionist asks: "Where do you come from?"

You take your time because you do not know what to answer. She keeps staring at you, with a firm look and firm glasses. Because you need forever to answer, she rewords her question: "For administrative reasons, what's your home country?"

You answer: "For administrative reasons, Romania."

You now live near the Danube, not in Romania, but in Germany. You do not want to be integrated, assimilated. Not if it means giving up on everything you were before moving here, shaking it off, leaving it behind, forgetting it, burying it. Your inner voice is a mixture of languages. Your life partner comes from Spain. Your best friend in Canada comes from Iran. There are many other languages inside you. Many cultures and ways of being in this world. How could you choose to only see one side of things when there are so many?

The paper that confirms that yes, you did live in the city where you did your PhD, claims that you were born in Timișoara, Bulgaria. For administrative reasons, within Europe, Romania and Bulgaria belong in the same bucket.

2015

I teach creative writing. I teach Canadians, Germans, and people from various other countries. I do this online. My teacher in Canada says: "What you want to express as a writer is not language, but something bigger that than, the thing beyond language." My teacher here says: "You need to have a very firm grasp of the language in which you write."

The Danube flows through many countries. Also through my home country. Also through this country that refuses to become my *Heimat*. That pulls away and does not allow me to hug it. That always maintains a proper distance between us through its language. There are many rules, but no intimacy.

I also write in English here, in a large company, and I can make a living with it. For as long as I wish. I am in a different tax category now than back when I was just a poor student who needed a visa. People talk to me differently. Especially in airports, when I wear suits and travel on business.

Every second year there is a Danube festival in town. There is food from all the countries on the Danube. Back when I was a child, the Danube in my home country was always hungry. She longed for blood. Between 1948 und 1989, hundreds of people tried to escape communistic Romania by crossing the Danube, by swimming to the Serbian side, back then Yugoslavia. Nobody knows how many made it to the other side and how many were brutally murdered in the process. But there is always someone who knows someone who survived.

My home country didn't treat the Danube-svabians well. I want to go running to all of them and start apologizing for everything my former countrymen did. Those who were lucky made it to a camp. They all had to sleep and pee together. Those who were the Germans in Romania were now the Romanians in Germany. They were accused of stealing. Even if they were Danube-svabians, they were still asked where they came from. Then they got a Nobel prize and both countries wanted to have them, but they belonged to neither. The Romanian Saxons also had to move to Svabia; Saxony was still in Eastern Germany when they escaped Romania.

It is a day in summer, a day like any other. Summer is coming to an end. It is the day I become a German citizen. Starting today, I am one of them. Yesterday, I was not. I don't really grasp what this means. As a writer, I am Canadian. The poetry however comes from Iran. As a lover, I am Spanish. As a cook, I am Indian. My child-heart remains Romanian. And everything else is nothing else but silence and a mixture of all those things that are something bigger than that, the thing beyond language.

The Shape of the Sky (I)

1. There are no stars in the Bremen-er sky. It is always gray and people here are old. I feel older than I am here, with nobody to hug or touch. For months I only touch money, plastic, furniture, nothing

that has life in it. Memories have become obsolete. I have become obsolete. Nobody knows me here. Nobody will, or at least this is what I feel. The sky line has been taken over by church gargoyles. In the fog before dawn, they look bigger and more medieval than they really are.

2. In Dortmund, we take a blanket with us and go to the park. We lie down on the grass. I rest my head against his armpit. I should feel safe in his arms but he's talking about death, evolution, and how meaningless life is. Again. People around us speak a language neither of us fully understands. I understand it better than he does, because at least I try. I can't see any stars in the sky. "Maybe we should break up," he says. I start weeping into his T-shirt, but I make no sound. If I stay like this, I can freeze time, and all I can hear is the grass grow underneath our bodies and feet. Later, we go on with our life together and pretend this has never happened.
3. Canadian skies, they seem so bright. There's snow in the sky too, the sky turns pink, and vanilla, and I forget to breathe, but the cold reminds me to. In Calgary, we walk to the place we call home. We carry our groceries. There is always a lot of snow and there is always a lot to carry. I should be paying more attention to my feet, but I always look at the sky. I see no stars. And we will not break up. I will not break up. My belly is heavy with the child we'll never have. It's been replaced by a giant ovarian cyst, but I don't fully know this yet.
4. The sky above the Niagara Falls. This is the sky that I'd like to share with someone. Instead, I take out a sheet of paper from my bag and I do what I always do: I turn the longing of the moment into poetry.

5. The sky seen from the terrace of the flat where I grew up. Eight years after leaving this place, I return. Coffee with my dad on the terrace just before sunrise. We take photos. Digital ones this time. Printed photos always smell of him, of home. Coffee always smells like home.
6. *Moldova Nouă*, near the Danube. The sun is setting down and I know that there are vipers on the dried out, hot hills behind the house where we are staying for the summer, the hills that lack trees. I am in my pre-teens. I want to share the orange of the sunset with someone, but all I can think about are the vipers, and the longing I feel in my loins. I am 12 and look older than I am, and can't decide what I want more: to watch and be and enjoy this sunset, or to share it with a boy.
7. The Danube again, this time at *Svinița*. Summer end. Childhood end. I have just turned 18. Down on my back, on a bench, in a park, with a young man's penis making its way into my mouth. This isn't how it's supposed to be. The full moon is high above us and there is nobody else around. I let my mind slip and fade away. He bites my neck and the birthmark on it until blood starts pouring out. I do not enjoy any of it but cannot find it within me to get up and leave. I am like a wooden doll pulled by strings. My eyes fixated on the dark sky.
8. We refuse to watch the sunset when it comes. Other couples do, at the Black Sea Shore, the sea into which the Danube keeps pouring. I am 21, the year before I move to Germany, and I am training myself to be on my own for long periods of time, in places where I do not know anyone, by taking long trips across Romania on my own. We refuse to watch the sunrise and we are not a couple anyway. The boy is younger than me, about to enter the last year of high-school. A minor I could corrupt if I wanted to. My hair is too short. I wish we kissed. Screw the sunrise! All we need is a pair of hands. And then it probably happens. The sunrise, not the kiss. We go back to the hotel, each of us to another room. Or

maybe I'm remembering it wrong. I think it was the same room, but different beds. A few years later, we will still send each other emails, but never again meet. A few nights later, a man his sister knows will touch my breasts through my night gown, against my will, when nobody is there to witness it. I tremble and keep pushing him away.

9. It's hard to see the clouds in this area. I'm at the Danube again, but closer to its springs. I live here now, in Ulm. It's hard to see any clouds because all I can see is fog. The tower of the minster, the tallest church steeple in the world as it may be, is nowhere to be found. But I trust my feet to know where they take me.
10. In my backyard in Ulm. With my 2 cats. The sky is almost clear. End of the day. The evening light spreads itself in playful shades on the wall of my neighbors' building. The shapes keep on changing.

The Cage (II)

Growing up, I used to believe, for a very long time, that I was the only person out there with a *mad* mother. I would have rather had alcoholic or divorced parents because that was something I could've at least talk about with my friends at school. There was no such thing as therapy or systemic therapy back then. There was only medication, and my father refusing to leave my mother like I sometimes asked him, begged him to, so that we could have a "normal" life. There was my anger, at him, at her, which came out in waves at times. There was only this and there were no choices. Not for me, at least.

Even decades later, in Romania, the subject of mental illness and mental health, the PTSD the whole country suffers from, the injustice done for decades to so many families, all of it remains taboo. Not only that but *we* still lack a compassionate, personal, nonclinical vocabulary around mental health and mental illness. We still lack a support system for children whose parents are mentally ill. We still lack family and systemic therapy. We lack school counseling. We lack someone to be there and tell such children, someone whose opinion they trust, that their parents' misery is not and has never been their fault. As a child, I lacked all of these things too. So I learned to comfort myself by reading and making up my own stories in order to live.

It takes me years, decades, to understand that my father, too, has always struggled with anxiety, a kind of restlessness, which worsens in his old age. It comes with a reluctance for change, with a need for things to stay as they are, to store things in our old home, and always keep them in the same place. I am not allowed, when I visit, to move things around, even slightly; everything has its own predefined place and his rules are to be followed strictly. He still tries to tell me what I am and am not allowed to do.

And then one day in 2021 I read one of his recent books, where, in an interview, he writes: "*Securitatea* remained like some sort of invisible *bau-bau* (scare) for decades after 1989." He writes about how, in the 1980s, he was forced to paint a portrait of Elena Ceaușescu for free, how *Securitatea* would come check on him each day until the commission was finished, how later his boss would threaten him and my mother with jail for withholding information from the state. "Luckily the Revolution came and they didn't take us," he tells me in May or June 2021. We talk a lot, about many things, but still not about everything that happened in communism.

The Cage (III)

In my childhood, my mother's friend who lives in Germany took me aside one day when she visited Romania with her husband and daughter and said: "You must accept that her state may not change. She might improve, but it may take years. Or she may stay like this for good." This woman's own daughter now has paranoid schizophrenia and is epileptic. They have very German-sounding names and they too escaped communism in the 80s. Back then, her daughter was healthy. Or at least not diagnosed. Germany was the heaven where everybody who escaped communism wanted to be. But their stories about the camp suck. It's where I now live, as an adult. It's where the sweets, sneakers, and other Easter presents came from back when I was a child. My mother has many cousins and they all have children and grandchildren. Almost all of them live in Germany. Germany is where, in 2004, at the age of 22, I move to study and start a scientific career. It is is where my uncle Tibi – my mother's second-degree cousin/the son of my grandfather's eldest brother – destroys his lungs by working long hours and night shifts in a factory in the cold. Not much different than my grandmother's experience in the 60s in Romania, but better paid. "I want to go home," his wife, Aunt Vera, tells me when I visit them in 2008. "For the last 16 years, I've felt like I've been away on vacation. And I cannot wait to go home. But we never go home. All we have is this feeling of being away. And when we are on vacation, for a few weeks each summer, then we finally go home." Another aunt, Olimpia, Tibi's sister, has Alzheimer's now and weighs just above 40 kg. She no longer recognizes anyone, but is always happy to get visits. At least this is what her granddaugther Anne tells me on FB. I have never met Anne in person, but my aunt used to tell me many stories about her and send me photos of them. Anne is young, under 30. She got married in the summer of 2016. She does not speak Romanian, we type in German over FB messenger. My German is still somewhat broken. This is the same Olimpia that my mother writes about back in 1994 – how she cooked and sew her a dress, while my mother was sleeping, back when they were young, my mother a young girl and Olimpia a teenager. This is the same Olimpia who writes me letters after I first move to Germany and sends me money behind her husband's back. The same Olimpia who tells me she has never fully embraced drawing. The same Olimpia who spends years learning about human psychology. An army of aunts and uncles that I no longer know, but who always know things about me, as my mother keeps in touch with everyone by phone and tells them everything about me. Sometimes, she changes details and adds layers of stories of her own to mine. Over time, this tendency of hers to make stuff up when she cannot remember all the details as they happened gets worse.

If You Want to Know Me

if you want to know me, don't ask me where I come from.
don't ask me whether my home country is nothing but black all over
my body. don't ask me questions about my body, about the endless
scars.

don't ask me about the nights under a violet fog in which you were
facing
the stars looking for complementary orange, and I the cold ground,
unable
to face the half-alive half-dead bodies dangling like hammocks
underneath
a sky in which nobody wanted to die.

your hope now carries the colors red, white, and blue, but mine is
covered
in dust particles and names of people I can no longer meet or trust.
underneath all that, it is still a pure, wild shade of green. the color of
hope
should not be split into two.

ask me about my childhood dreams and I will ship them to you, ask
me
how many of them came true, please, oh, please, don't give me labels,
or
call me names, don't split me from you.

and if you'd ask me all that, I'd tell you that only one came true.
and that is more than some people have in one hundred trips
around the sun, moon, and stars.

the sun was yellow, then indigo. we could not tell pirates from mermaids,
riding the waves, faces pressed into one another. even at the shore,
the waves kept moving, slower, faster.

if you want to know me, sit with me inside this human temple
I built for you out of the scar tissue of all our ancestors,
passed from generation to generation
into all of me and all of you.

sit with me and tell me stories in rediscovered or invented languages, until
your tears find shelter inside my chest and my right ventricle finds a land
of kisses around your temples. until our hearts become rainbows that melt
into one another as only homes can do.

Old Age

Mirror (II)
Aging

I am in my early 30s and live far away from it all. Whenever I visit my parents, my mother says: "You've changed, you've turned rough and mean." My father tells her: "You may not like what she's saying, but it's the truth." I shrug my shoulders: "I'm being pragmatic, that's all."

The man I love tells me: "You are so warm and tender. So giving." One day, he tells his therapist: "I no longer recognize myself in the mirror." Prozac is what she prescribes. "Don't leave me," he says. I want to, but don't. One day, I am sick. The next day, he is gone. I relive this story again and again with different men. With a gay male artist who later becomes a friend, I make plaster masks of my face. Each mask has flaws.

"I am so tired," I tell my doctor. He prescribes levothyroxine for my thyroid and vitamin D. "The drugs should cure everything," he says. "Will they cure loneliness too?" I want to ask him, but don't. I take my drugs each morning and hope.

My mother calls me in the middle of the night and says: "Your father is sick, he turned blue last night, his hands clasped around the remote control, and around my hand. I couldn't unclench his hands. He squezeed my hand so hard, I started crying. The ER guys managed to remove my hand from his. The ambulance took him away, with the remote control in his hand. He cannot talk. When he can, he's hallucinating. He has asked me twice if I am there for Daddy's funeral. But it's not clear whose Daddy. Does he mean his father, who has long been gone? Or does he mean himself, and thinks that I am you? He's been having convulsions all day."

By phone, I ask my friends to go see him in shifts. "Hurry," my friends say, "it won't be long." It is Sunday. I book the first flight I can get. I pack black clothes. Cash, for the funeral. A friend takes my 2 cats to a so-called cat hotel. I pay double than usual, due to the short notice, a special offer. On the way to the airport, I buy postcards, of impressionist paintings.

In that hospital in the corrupted land I left behind me years ago, where nurses need constant bribing, where having a health insurance is of no use, because one must pay for everything anyway, I become my father's watcher, his mother, and his wife. I do all the things that my mother won't, can't do. He cannot talk but his eyes follow my face, he caresses my hand with his (there are needles sticking out of it), and looks at the images I bring him. With a finger he points to the wall. There's a painting there too. Irises, by Van Gogh. They are our favorite flowers. A few days later, he starts to speak again. On the way to the MRI I tell him not to be afraid. "I'm no longer afraid," he manages to whisper. "Not anymore." He cannot walk, other people move him around, lifting him on bedsheets from one bed to another, cleaning after him (if I pay them often enough, they do). At times, he seems painfully aware of what's going on. I no longer know what to wish for him.

At home, I once again become my mother's mother. She is afraid that he'll die. Afraid that he won't and that she won't be able to watch over him. That he won't walk or talk again. That she'll be alone. That she will mix up her medication, forget how to cook. Forget to feed and wash herself. It has happened before.

I lift the bed covers under which she's hiding. I yell at her, like I used to do back in my childhood: "Get up! Eat! Help me! I can't do this alone!"

In their home, she leaves no room for my fear. And all I want is to press reset and be 5 years old.

While my father is still in hospital and I have to return to my golden German cage, I get my father a physiotherapist and he slowly learns to walk again.

I am in my mid 30s. I live alone, still far away from my parents. I send them money. My father keeps getting sick, again and again. I visit. There's no place left to call home. On the nights when I manage to fall asleep, I keep waking up. Panic attacks. My head won't stop spinning. I can't drive. I have heart burn and many other inexplicable digestive problems. My liver enyzmes go through the roof and stay there for several years. My doctor reduces my levothyroxine dose but does not do more.

A friend my own age dies alone in her flat. Her name was Diana. They find her days later, her baby next to her, unfed. Incineration is what they go for. Cheapest option, chosen for her by the German state, as she didn't have a family to look after her.

Who knows where her baby is now. Son of a refugee, vanished, and an immigrant mother, dead. A boy who will not know his past. For a split second I consider adopting him. But how would I raise a little boy on my own?

I feel like I grew up too fast. I am 36 years old now. I don't have a partner and don't know if I'll ever have children. If I want children. And if I'll have my 3 fibroids removed. Meanwhile they keep on growing.

My father now paints at home, while my mother sleeps. Climbing the 3 floors to his sudio has become a challenge, but once, when I visit, we take a taxi, and go there. The door of his studio is white. I can barely trace our old colorful drawings underneath the surface.

My mother keeps getting better, then worse, between my father's uncontrollable crises. We now know that what he has is hyponatremia. We all do our best to keep things under control.

When he's well, he cuts my mother's thin gray hair. If I'm there, I comb it. "I used to have such beautiful hair," she says. "Yes, like fire, but in a good way," I tell her. Her old portrait is still in my room, like in my childhood, but on a different wall.

My gynecologist tells me it's time, that with my fibrous uterus, I shouldn't wait any longer – it's either now or never. I got my fibrous uterus from my mother. Yet, she still had me. She struggled a lot to make and keep me in her belly until I was ready to face the world, but she pulled it off, because she really wanted a baby, a girl. But I don't want children, a husband, a new family. I have more than enough responsibility as it is. And still 10 or more years to go before I reach my own early menopause, like my mother has. This is what I most fear.

And here I am now, all on my own. My parents far away, counting the moments they still have left each day. Drugs can't cure everything. The passing of time. Aging. Death. A lack of connection. To people, to places. I'm still my father's daughter, sometimes his mother, and more. I fought so hard, for so long, to unbecome my mother, to become her opposite. To become that young, strong, independent person that my father so badly wanted me to become. But these days, when I look in the mirror, I am no longer sure. I really don't know anymore. Where my mother ends and I begin.

Am I (Like) My Mother?

Where do I begin? Where do I begin to begin? Begin to tell her story? And to what extent is her story hers? How much of it is my grandfather's story? And in a collectivist oppressive culture, how much of his story has he ever truly owned? I can't even do this honestly in our mother tongue. But before I begin, our words blend and melt into none. I will begin wherever I can. As long as the story is told. For I, for we, for the next generation – if there will be one – cannot carry the burden of its weight anymore.

Body (I)

Some years ago, I heard that we carry our ancestors' trauma in our genes and pass it on to the next generations. My body remembers better than I do. It remembers what my mother's body remembers.

Together, our bodies remember many things from our shared past and sometimes, there are so many memories that our individual bodies – unlike those of animals – don't remember how to shake off the trauma. So we store it instead.

I forget to remember myself. I make up stories instead. Stories I share with the world. It's like going through old sets of slides, slicing life, my life, as if it belonged to somebody else.

My body still remembers to seek freedom, through motion in time and space, through words, words I tell myself and the world until they make sense.

I had never expected to find my grandfather in a poem that he wrote decades ago, before my existence even became a possibility. It's only there, in his writing, that I can now discover his voice.

There is also a distorted voice in the secret police files we can now acccess, a voice that isn't really his.

Now, I am writing the story that he couldn't tell, the story that my mother couldn't finish.

We write to survive. We become the stories we tell.

My story is larger than my body. I am just the vessel that carries it.

Silenced (III)

Twenty years before I was born, on a day that changed the course of many lives, my grandfather – whom I've never met face-to-face – was imprisoned by the (back then) ruling Communist Party. Twelve years after I was born, my mother entered an early menopause and was diagnosed as having bipolar disorder (or manic-depressive disorder, as it was called then), a diagnosis she shares with a number of family members.

My grandfather was arrested for expressing an "unfriendly attitude" towards the ruling and only political party of our country in the 50s. At the rise of communism, intellectuals were seen as dangerous, as disturbing social elements. He was a notary, a poet, someone who helped a lot of Jewish families during WWII by giving them fake papers, fake names. He was someone who had German friends in the Banat area, with whom he openly discussed national and international politics, something that in the end got him arrested.

Around the time of her diagnosis, my mother tries to tell his story. I read it 25 years later.

Stories repeat themselves. Words and thoughts repeat themselves. I play it all in my head, again and again, trying to find who I am, why I am the way I am, trying to find meaning.

Arrest. Prison. No news. Absence. "Unhealthy political background." Divorce. No studies for the girls. Not at first. Later. After the mock divorce. Eventually.

(Beating. Famine. Broken spleen.)

Early liberation.

The Great Expectations. The movie, which they watched together – she, her sister, and him – at the cinema after he was sent back home.

Then, a diagnosis: leukemia.

Four months in hospital. Ten blood transfusions. A fake death certificate: pneumonia.

Forty more years of communism and above all: silence. Numbing silence. Walls have eyes. So we all just go on keeping silent. We get extremely good at it.

Before prison, things happened too. My grandfather wrote about his brother's life and the events that led to his suicide. He did it for us, their family. His brother married a woman who exploited him. He feared imprisonment at the rise of communism in Romania. He was kind and weak. I assume that he had undiagnosed depression. He pulled a knife through his heart, down by the train tracks, on Serbian New Year's Eve.

What the brother feared is what my grandfather lived first hand. My grandfather's secret police files, which we only get a hold of in 2011, show that his brother was also part of the same collective investigation as my grandfater, at least in the beginning.

My mother tries to write down her father's story when she gets sick. There are many events there, his arrest and all the milestones that followed. There's nostalgia, loss, and anger. My mother thinks that she's still being followed. By communists, by the KGB. She writes that those who wish to understand communism should look not only at the 1989 revolution, but also at its roots, and the impact it had on so many generations.

There are stories of the old ways of life there. Stories of our family's history that I would otherwise not know. Days in the countryside, visiting relatives. Moments from my childhood in which my mom is deliberately trying to create a bond between me and her father, from her perspective. To preserve his story, his memory. The story that could not be told before. She's the link between us. A broken link.

Towards the end, my mother's words become less structured, more repetitive, more sentimental. But before that happens, her writing is sharp and clear.

She writes that while her body goes on living, her soul lies next to her father's, in his coffin, for good. She refers to his soul as being up in Heaven, with God.

She calls my father her guardian angel. She calls me a living doll. She refers to her family as a tree, and to my grandfather as its trunk. Its strongly hit, chopped down trunk. Does my mother and her whole side of the family suffer from survivor's guilt?

Like me, she studied Chemistry, although (like me), what she would've liked to do was study Literature and Writing. A lot of her diary entries outline the books she liked to read as a child, or those she received as presents.

After months of writing frenetically, listening to loud music, talking about being followed and pregnant, she collapses into a depression that lasts 10 years, before it turns again into mania. She stops eating and washing herself. She loses weight very fast, because she is starving herself, and, on some days, she talks about killing herself. Her psychotherapist, whom she only meets once with no results, tells my father that she has never before seen such a reluctant patient.

My mother is too afraid to talk about what happened because she trusts nobody.

As my mother enters her bipolar menopause, I am just hitting puberty.

When my mother was 12, she lost her father. When I was 12, I lost my mother. She was still there, physically, but like a ghost. She would get up early in the morning, stand up, and fall next to the bed. I would pick her up and put her back to sleep, then go to school, as if everything was fine and we were a "normal" family.

She only comes out of her depression when I move out. Ten years later, when I am 22. Before my aunt (my mother's sister) dies (of too late diagnosed metastatic brain cancer, after a 3-week coma), she tells me: "Don't have children, your genetic material is too heavy." She also tells me not to adopt, as there is no way to fully know what trauma and medical history children inherit.

On my father's side of the family, there is also a lot of mental illness. My half-sister, from his first marriage, 21 years older than me, is under permanent care, diagnosed with severe paranoid schizophrenia in her early adulthood. She was a brilliant student before that. Her failed suicide attempt happened soon after. Two of my father's uncles committed suicide; both used guns. One of them was only 16. These are things many people know about our family but it is not customary to discuss them in public. We have a saying in Romania: "Don't wash your dirty laundry in public." So I never talk about them growing up. I would not even know how. We do not really have the vocabulary to frame them.

Years later, my father says about my aunt that she was also bipolar, but used all kinds of drugs to medicate herself. Once she was allowed to study (but only at the special part-time evening program), she went from being a nurse to being a psychotherapist. A children psychotherapist.

Before my aunt dies, she also tells me things about her life. How she's always been a caretaker. It is she who took care of my grandmother in her old age. It is she who married a man who retired early due to mental illness.

I am only 19 when my aunt dies, not without giving me that warning though, and I start wondering if anyone from my parents' generation is really sane. And I know one thing: I don't wish to become my aunt. She tells me with a painful awareness that she gave and gave, but has never felt completed by another human being. After my grandfather's arrest, as the eldest sister and an adult, she had to get a job and for years worked as a nurse. She worked and later helped my father and me take care of my mother, her younger sister. And later, of their mother, when my mother could not do it.

When I am in the second year of my BSc studies, my mother sleeps her way through her sister's terminal illness and funeral. Because we can't make her eat, and because of her drugs' side effects, she sometimes hallucinates. My father continuously refuses to hospitalize my mother and pretends that everything is just fine.

During the same month, I take and pass exams with impeccable grades as if everything were "just fine." I am known and appreciated for my humor, my wit, my positive ways of being in the world. But at home, all I see is my mother's helplessness and hallucinations. And all I can think about, on most days, is escape.

In late 2005, my cousin fights with my parents over inheritance. For my mother, this is a trigger. She has another maniacal episode, the first one since her initial collapse. She writes frenetically, once again, about my grandfather. About communism. She stops taking her medication. She spends money, prays, and doesn't sleep. She says she has God and prayer and doesn't need medicine. She can't handle the pressure.

Then, she falls into depression again.

Six years later, my cousin moves to Sweden. Just before that, 50 years after my grandfather's arrest, my cousin gets the secret police files about our grandfather from Bucharest. 605 pages of "collective investigation."

More family members get diagnosed with depression, a diagnosis later changed to bipolar disorder.

This is our family's disease. Our century-long silencing and the way our bodies are fighting it. The rise and fall of an oppressive system. The words coming out to tell the needed story.

My grandfather loved words, their cadence, their power. He knew their power. And those who silenced him knew it too. Even now, my mother needs and wants to speak about what happened, but is too afraid. She tells me to be careful about what I share and with whom. And yet, I know that this is what we all need. To get the story out into the world, to claim its truth, our truth.

All my life I've wanted to give voice to the silenced ones. I only recently realized how much of that silence lived in my family, and how deteriorating and deadly such silencing can be.

I didn't know that all I had to do was take a closer look at myself. At my mother, at my grandfather. I carry their stories within me, and ever since he's been silenced – his words, our words – have been struggling to come out and meet the daylight.

Shared Spaces (I)

My mother is giving birth, but not to me. While she is connected to machines and there is poison dripping into her veins, I feel her pain inside my own body, and it feels just like getting my period, but larger. I don't know why there are no doctors around, and why my father isn't there. I am the age I was when she gave birth to me. Sometimes I cannot tell who is in that bed, she or I, because it is me experiencing all the sensations, in my body, but looking in on her from the outside. And I know in this moment that I do not feel the magic of giving birth. I know that I dread the hours that will come, the machines beeping and pumping, the sweat on the bed sheets, and not knowing when all this will end, how long it will last. I also know that this is a form of disassociation, but also of association. I know that there will be a lot of blood. I know that right here, right now, inside this room, I am my mother, while she is falling asleep. I want to see what we will give birth to, and whether it will be a monster. I wake up and write about this monster we carry within us, this pain. I can only write my mother's story when I am away from her and from her pain as she feels it to this day. I can only finish this text when I do not see her suffering reflected hour after hour into myself. This isn't how my mother needs to be loved, but this is the only way I know.

The Typewriter
1985

I'm 3 years old. I take out my lined notebooks and "write"; my "words" and "sentences" are signs, symbols, random scribbles. I do not know the letters of the alphabet yet, but I structure my scribbles like paragraphs. I do this all summer long.

1987

I discover my mother's typewriter, capital letters, my name, her name, my father's name. I love the sound that the metal letters make when hitting the paper and leaving their mark there. At work, my mother has another typewriter, but I don't use that one much.

1994

On that same typewriter on which I learn to articulate our names, my mother starts writing her father's story. The story isn't made up. It's a story she still can't live with.

2019

"How come you were allowed to own typewriters back then?" I ask my parents when I visit them in summer.

Because I have recently read Carmen Bugan's book *Burying the Typewriter*, I now know that all privately owned typewriters had to be registered with the Police back in communism. My parents tell me that they were expected (like all other typewriter owners) to type the standard text given by the Police on their respective typewriter(s) each year, then hand it over to the Police. The Police would then check that no anticommunism flyers were being spread with those exact fonts. I don't remember any childhood conversation in my family starting with: "We are going to the Police." Everything was done in secret, even if there was nothing to hide, even if in theory none of us was under surveillance, at least not then, at least not to our knowledge. My parents tell me they sold the typewriter in the 90s. I board a plane from Timișoara to Munich 2 hours after this conversation. I write down these words freely, on a phone that looks like any other phone. One on which characters have no signature.

2021

Throughout the pandemic, I visit my father twice. The first time, to bury my mother. The second time, to celebrate his 82nd birthday. I am in quarantine the second time, so I spend a lot of time at home.

In our storage room, there are a lot of spider webs, there is a lot of dust. Everything is there. My father's old paintings, still in good shape. The doll my mother got from my grandfather in the midst of the 1950s financial crisis and passed down to me.

My mother's old typewriter. Heavy, in a gray bag, tied with a dark blue knot. I take it out. The ink is dry but the typewriter can be restored. At least I think so.

My father corrects me: "No, this wasn't your mother's, she had a bigger one, Olimpia. We sold that one. This one was mine. But you cannot find the black thread you need anymore." Then he goes to one of the many drawers in our house that store so many things, things I may not even be aware of, and pulls one out. It's as old as the typewriter, from 1980, and somehow, still there.

The nested dolls, which I would play with through my childhood at *Mica*'s place, are gone, but all the memories about my family are there, untouched by time. My father and I still share them, and more.

When I return to my German home after one month with him, one of the first things I do is buy a new typewriter. It is soft pink and called *We R Memory Keepers*.

Acacia

Munich, Germany, 2018. Here, far away from everything that has happened and is still happening over there, here very close to my street (I have recently moved to a small street, a new street that has only recently officially been registered with the City of Munich), here on a parallel street not far from my own, I can watch the acacia trees grow and bloom, I can hear the noise made by the trams passing by. Just like in my childhood, in that place far away. And it is strange, how much it matters to have, or at least to have had a past. To once have had a home, a physical and emotional space called home, some time, far away, a long time ago, deep somewhere in our personal history, on a sepia background rather than a colorful or black-and-white one. When photographic films could hardly be bought, but your father made and developed photos at home, in the bathtub, overnight. I could insert a quote from Mircea Eliade here, one about the magic universe of the childhood which, once left behind, becomes a myth. It can never again be found as it once was. Or one from Emil Cioran, the nihilist philosopher who spent his exile in France, about his lost paradise, the village with its goats and graveyards, from the time before he started going to school in the city. Perhaps we all have a moment, around the age of 12, when we start becoming hybrids, trapped somewhere between childhood and our teenage years, still at the disposal of our parents, who make decisions for us, even when they can no longer do it for ourselves, because of absence. The absence can take many shapes. It can be caused by illness, by arrest, by death. Sometimes we can best characterize its place by absence. By the things or people that are no longer there. The absence makes place for new presences: of fears, of thoughts, of darkening. Of rebirth. The night my grandfather died, his chair remained empty, this time for good. The dog Lordi cried of grief all night.

—~—

I would watch her from outside, the little girl
Who'd come to the window each night,
Tell me goodnight stories
And eat my blooms.
I gave her shade as the sun shone bright in summer.
I gave their whole home shade with my trunk and branches.
Her mother would sometimes come to the window too,

At least the window of her own room,
If not the one in her daughter's.
One summer, when the girl was 12,
Part of me died.
First, there was a night with thunder and lightning,
Then came the men with hatchets.
It was safer that way, they said,
The rest of me would not fall onto their home and strangle it.
Everything changed from that day onwards.
On some days, from my shortened height,
I'd still see the girl's shade lingering
Above what was left of me,
But almost never her mother's.
I sprouted new leaves and short branches years later,
But I don't know if I'll ever sprout new blooms.
The little girl grew up.
I'd see her leave the house on her own
And then the street, and probably the city, the country.
Years passed, and my roots grew stronger.
And when the woman-girl comes visit,
She still looks at me, if only for a second.
With her hands, her camera, and her pen.
With her memory and her imagination.
She both looks and doesn't look like her mother.
On some days, I think she writes about us.

The Girl and Her Journey

The girl thought she had choices that she could rationally choose from. Ignoring her calling. Ignoring whom she loved, or at least felt drawn to. Ignoring her needs to place those of other people first.

There were so many things inside and around her womb that were not supposed to be there: fibroids, cysts, precancerous cells. Most of these things grew because of others, not because of herself. Or, with some she was born. All could be cut out (to make room for a baby, that was the dream, or, at least, her doctor's dream) and, after their removal, there were scars. The scars took a long time to heal. Those who took the longest did not leave a trace of blood. She lost parts of her former self on the surgery table, parts that were weighing her down and weren't really herself.

At the last surgery, the one meant to prevent or at least slow down the development of cervical cancer, the narcosis doctor asked her about her last vacation.

"I don't remember," she said at first, but then she continued: "It was at Zürcher See."

"And, did you swim?" he asked her.

"No," she answered, "it was too cold; it was winter."

She knew what he was doing, making conversation until the narcosis cocktail will have made its way from the vein in her right arm into her brain.

"Nobody can swim in that lake," he told her, "except for 2 months in summer."

And then she told him: "I think I will now fall asleep."

It was a sleep without dreams, there were no whales to be followed to the bottom of the ocean. Unlike in the dreams she used to have years ago, when everything was heavy and so many things were said out loud in anger, yet so many other things remained untold.

When she woke up, the sun was out and
she needed almost no pain medication.

—∞—

I write the story of a magical girl who doesn't have a mother but is always put in the position of helping others, of mothering others.

When they need her, they want her around them. Later, she is no longer wanted and she has to go. She reminds me of Shel Silverstein's *The Giving Tree*. A poem I grow to love and hate over time.

—~—

Empathy is my greatest power. I still struggle with feeling it for myself. Empathy lets me understand what is not said. It helps me understand the pain and wants of others. It helps me help them get what they want. But it is also, at times, a measure of poor boundaries. Of poor self-care. Of reminding myself constantly "me first." Of no longer placing my mother's pain before my own. It takes me years to unlearn this and a number of failed romantic relationships and toxic friendships. I learn to say no and to walk away without looking back. I still look back sometimes, with some sort of unfulfilled longing. But also, I learn to say yes to myself.

This all sounds cheesy. Like something you read on the internet looking for inspirational quotes. Except that it is our life. My life. Day after day, one foot after another.

I learn to unweigh myself of other people's problems.

On some days, I do it better than on others.

With some people, I do it better than with others.

My empathy remains bigger than my pain.

—~—

It will never happen. Going back in time. This is why I try to write this book as much as possible in the present. So that somewhere, sometime, certain things are still happening, in the present moment. And perhaps, perhaps, they can be undone. Maybe even a little. I want the good things to keep happening. I want to freeze the part before things turned bad. But if I do this too well, if I do it perfectly, the bad things will also stay locked forever. And perhaps time isn't linear, but cyclical. At least in our memory. At least in our imagination. And aren't memory and imagination so often the same thing?

—~~—

I cannot write linearly about life, my life, other people's lives, the way things happened. I never cared much about numbers, facts. I cared more about the meaning they carry. Not in a vacuum, but to specific people. I am not a historian, but I am a scientist. I believe in objective truths. But I also know how subjective truths may completely and radically change our perception of reality and, most importantly, of ourselves.

—~~—

Sometimes our power is taken away from us. But there are also times when we have as much power as we think we have. When we give up our power because we feel threatened by another, we lose a little of ourselves. We give in to self-hate. We let self-hate take over the best of us. Our lack of power is often temporary. We have more of it than we think we do. Unless we live in a dictatorship. One of the things that most annoys me in Germany is how little people believe in their own power to make a difference. In the workplace nobody complains openly to their superior. What will my boss think if I do this? Nobody wants to risk taking responsibility for their concerns, for their wishes.

I do.
I get into trouble.
I get kicked out of groups.
I am told to calm down.
At work, I am told to stop being so negative.
"You can think it, but do not say it out loud".
Is this democracy?

—~—

Once, I almost get fired, like my mother once.
And once, another time, I do.

—~—

Yet, I am still here. Still hoping, talking, dreaming, calling people out. Calling them by their names. Doing the work that needs to be done. Speaking my truth. If, by writing these words, I can make someone's life more bearable, I am not doing this – all these hours spent alone writing, editing, reading, daydreaming – in vain. I want to be the person I didn't have at my side when I was growing up and my mother had depression. Sometimes we have to be our own mothers. In her novel *Motherhood,* Sheila Heiti writes that the hardest thing sometimes is not become a mother to anyone, ever. I think it is impossible. As teacher, trainer, friend, lover – it is impossible. When my parents grew old and helpless, I found myself forced to turn into their mother. Until I just couldn't do it anymore and I had to take a step back.

—~—

Last week I watched *Als Hitler das rosa Kaninchen stahl* and it was everything I needed to see that night. The movie is a lot of things, but there is this one scene set in rural Switzerland (the first country where Anna and her family are refugees), when Anna goes to school for the first time. She walks happily and confidently through the middle of the classroom to the seat assigned to her (the one still empty) and all the other children in her class laugh. "She doesn't know," they say, "it is not her fault." "Know what?" she asks the other children. "Girls are not allowed to walk in the middle of the classroom. Only the boys are allowed in the middle. Girls have to walk on the side." She is only a little girl, but she keeps defying the roles that others try to impose on her throughout the movie. The first book I ever read on my own, front to back, was *Heidi, Girl of the Alps*. Most of it also takes place in Switzerland. Heidi's mother dies when she is a little girl. She lives with her grumpy grandfather at first, then later with an invalid little girl in Frankfurt, in Germany. In the Alps, she's happy eating cheese with the goats.

My Voice (II)

The Angry Voice

You say I have rough edges
because I embrace my anger
when it comes splashing out in all its colors,
the anger that rises all the way
into my mouth,
into the world,
into the mouths of others.
It's the kind of anger
I refuse to censor.
It's the kind of anger
that is needed
to know true softness.
It's the kind of anger
that generations before me
could not release
without being thrown
behind bars.
So yes, when it rises,
I refuse to stop it from turning into words,
when over and over again
you feel entitled

to restrict my freedom,
to violate my boundaries,
to tell me how and what to think.
I am rough, as much as I am gentle.
I am strong in my vulnerability.
My voice is a muscle
and there's nothing worse than not using it.

The Singing Voice

Munich. February 2019. A small room with lots of people. My 3 fibroids finally removed only 2 weeks ago, together with 2 polyps, my belly still an open wound. A medical warning: "You could die if you get pregnant in the next 6 months, your uterus would not be able to handle it."

"I am here to heal," I say. "I used to sing so much in the past. And then, there are my ancestors. I want to create healing for them too. I want to send a ripple of love back in time, both into the past and into the future. Into myself. I am a skeptic," I tell them (I seem to be one of the few non-hippies here, all dressed in black, limited in motion to my chair, which I need because I cannot stand for too long yet), "but I am open to whatever is going to happen here this weekend."

And then we sing. It has been ages since I have sang in what appears to be a choir. We don't know the lyrics of the song, but it doesn't matter. We hum. Our voices blend into one voice. Something is rising inside me, a heat spreading upwards, invading my chest, head, and arms. My body warms up and tears gather in my eyes. It's not winter, but I'm a child dancing in the snow, twirling and catching snowflakes on the tip of my tongue.

There's no need for words or different voices today. There's room for us all, for this song we create together without being too busy about the singer. This morning is both soft and intense, a meditation. I feel both exposed and safe. I don't want to leave this space.

The weekend-long *Voice Odyssey* workshop is taking off. Although my womb is very much a tender, open wound and I am constrained to my chair for most of these 2 days, I can feel, already as we start, that I have come home again, into my body, into my voice, into a space of sharing my wounds and my joys with others.

The Romanian Singing Voice

Lume, lume, soro lume! (EN "World, world, sister world!")

Maria Tănase, Romania's Edith Piaf, is the voice mine sounds a lot like. I remember going to watch Adriana Trandafir play her at my old high-school in my home town. My voice that is so much deeper when I sing than when I speak. Unless I give it weight on purpose when I speak. *Lume, lume, soro lume!*

This balkanic mix of melancholy and joy of life is what I miss the most. And then there is the *lasă-mă să te las* mentality which I hate the most. I remember being new in Germany, a freshly arrived foreigner – a word I had never associated with myself before moving here – and missing the intensity of Romanian life, with all its pros and cons. In Germany everything was still, sterile, in isolation. Or perhaps this is how life in Germany felt to me, not to "them" - the "real" Germans.

The real danger of being labeled "foreigners" is that we become foreigners to ourselves. One day, the estrangement simply happens. You look into the mirror and at photos of yourself and they do not match anymore. You haven't aged but you've gained weight and that makes you look older. You can no longer claim what other people like referring to as beauty.

Lume, lume, soro lume!

The Writing Voice

Throughout all the chaos in my life, there has always been a constant. The world of words. Not all books offered me the connection I longed for. Some lacked intimacy. Or I lacked the knowledge, the vocabulary at least, to uncover what I was longing for: a deeper meaning, a deeper insight into the human soul.

I attract men who lack empathy: narcissists, psychopaths, autists. I let them have it. Most of the times I do. But I have boundaries now. I draw clear lines. And sometimes I just turn my back and walk away. Narcissistic abuse. One of them says we are all narcissists.

There is always a beginning and an end. Or perhaps there isn't. We move around in circles trying to make sense of things. Yet some doors remain locked. But it isn't always the ones that should stay locked. There are doors I wish to unlock but can't.

In this story I am trying to tell, I both lost and found myself. It is costing me years of my life, of looking on the inside instead of looking out. Of watching my parents age, of watching myself lose and gain weight. Of witnessing the age of Trump and fake news rising. Of witnessing neonazism in Germany rising. Of witnessing 30 years since the Romanian revolution. Of witnessing a new self taking shape.

Of watching *Als Hitler das rosa Kaninchen stahl* and learning about girls that are supposed to walk on the side instead of in the middle of the classroom but who refuse to play along. First because they do not know about the rules and later because they do, but choose to ignore them. Choose not to follow them.

Of watching the *Orlando* exhibition curated by Tilda Swinton at the *Literaturhaus* in München. Of standing face-to-face with the words written by Virginia Woolf, in her own handwriting. Of reading the words of the curator on the landscape of *Orlando* being much more than a book about the flexibility of gender, about it being a book about "true freedom from the imperatives of nationality, of history, and of class, as well as of gender (...) a story about the life and development of a human striving to become liberated from the constructs of prescriptive (...) norms of any kind. To consider this story's limitlessness, its sense of innate and empowered boxlessness.

To consider the wider territories of identity, of dream, of heredity, of consciousness, of memory, of history, of fantasy, of the limitations of mortality, of life itself. To consider the consolation of the wilderness of the future, this was the call to the artists in this show."

Virginia Woolf is one of my biggest writerly influences. I read *Orlando* for the first time when I was 13 and *The Waves* when I was 16. I didn't understand all their nuances back then but I felt touched, stimulated, intrigued. I didn't know back then that it was "allowed" to write like this. Breaking the rules of gender and of genre, turning poetry into prose. I took asiduos notes of quotes that I came back to over the years. I've reread both books many times since then, and many others.

I discover her work, her early loss of her mother, as mine sinks into the depth of depression in my pre-teen years. I am perhaps too young for her books, but I don't care. I go to the *International House* and there is a lot of information there, about her work, about her life. About her lifelong struggle with depression and her ultimate suicide. I read *The Waves* and *Orlando* over and over again, write down quotes, which I revisit over the years. She becomes someone like an impossible mother to me. Someone who both is and isn't like my mother. *A woman who forgot to dream but became a dream herself.* A woman who, despite her depression, was able to also be a writer. A female role model, unlike the many male models in Romanian literature.

As a culture, Romanians are predisposed to melancholia. Our most beloved poets are romantics (our national poet Mihai Eminescu), symbolists (with a predisposition towards death and decay topics – George Bacovia), dying violently in their youth (Nicolae Labiș), or alcoholic dreamers bending language (Nichita Stănescu).

I believe we read to be seen. When I was growing up and found myself reading Virginia Woolf's and, later, Anaïs Nin's controversial diaries and novels, I felt seen and understood, much more than I when I was reading Romanian literature. It is Anaïs Nin who, through her diaries, taught me that personal writing is powerful, that there are ways to be in this world that defy conventional marriage, that a woman can choose not to birth children, that life and writing are made of key moments and the rest is just filling, and that the inner life lived fully makes all the difference. I felt it as a tall shy teenager with budding writerly aspirations and I feel it now. And they gave me a standard to aspire to as a writer. To read Tilda Swinton's words on curating the *Orlando* exhibition, her message to the contributors, made me once again feel deeply human and unalone.

The Free Voice

I'm fascinated by this idea of our deepest wound being both our weakness and our source of power; of how we inherit the wound, of how it becomes (part of) us – sometimes even the core of our identity – and at the same time generative of something else, larger than our isolated, individual stories. If we integrate our trauma. There is nothing I could have done to save myself from this story of me. It was longing to be told. It is born out of pain and love. Isn't everything born out of love?

I am not wanted. But my voice is no longer breakable. It isn't marginal and it isn't at the center. It isn't privileged but it is also no longer oppressed, not like my grandfather's was. My voice is here to stay, to awaken, to shutter, to whisper, to love, to draw attention, to scream: "The Emperor is naked, don't you see?" I am here to speak up, and with my voice, to make waves. And room, for a new kind of underrepresented voices to grow. To be seen. And heard. And hated. And loved.

Story (EN)

This story isn't only mine,
My body is just the portal that carries it.
It is born from everything we kept locked
For far too long in our bodies.

It is born from the scorched earth
That was buried deep down
Under the trees in the forest,
Under the dried out water.

Lift this weight off my shoulders,
Lift this weight from inside my body,
You, wind flowing at sunset
With the ravens, into the horizon.

What remains is only a faded memory
Whispered around the fire, when night falls,
As a warning, to children by elders,
Until it becomes legend.

Poveste (RO)

Povestea asta nu e doar a mea,
Trupul meu e doar portalul care o poartă.
E născută din toate lucrurile închistate
Mult prea îndelung în trupurile noastre.

E născută din pământul ars,
Din pământul săpat adânc
Sub copacii din pădure,
Sub apa secetată.

Ia această povară de pe umerii mei,
Ia această povară din trupul meu,
Tu, vânt ce plutești la apus
Cu corbii, înspre orizont.

Ce rămâne e doar o amintire estompată,
Șoptită în jurul focului, la ceas de seară,
Ca o avertizare, copiiilor de către bătrâni,
Până când devine legendă.

The Pandemic

The Shape of the Sky (II)

RO „Cine iubește și lasă,
Cine iubește și lasă,
Dumnezeu să-i dea pedeapsă,
Dumnezeu să-i dea pedeapsă.
Târâișul șarpelui
Și pasul gândacului,
Vâjâitul vântului,
Pulberea pământului."

EN "He who loves and leaves,
He who loves and leaves,
May God punish him,
May God punish him.
With the crawling of the snake,
The step of the cockroach,
Roaring of the wind,
Dust of the earth."

DE „Wer liebt und verläßt,
Wer liebt und verläßt,
Den soll Gott strafen,
Den soll Gott strafen.
Mit dem Kriechen der Schlange,

Mit dem Schritt des Käfers,
Dem Surren des Windes,
Dem Staub der Erde.

Excerpt from a traditional Romanian love (curse) song

What I know or think I know for sure:

- a lot of things are in the air, but cannot be seen
- memory is like the sky
- maps and neighbors are love and connection
- water is everywhere: underneath the ground, but also in the sky, as vapors, snow, and clouds
- many things are hidden but they are also in plain sight, just underneath the surface of the wound
- birth, childhood, partnerhood, motherhood, aging, and death are inescapable
- many things continue to be carried despite their heaviness because letting go can be harder at times; who knows what'll happen once we let go
- memory and forgetting can be very much alike
- stories of good and bad times are often merged
- this story I'm trying to tell is larger than my own body; my body is only the vessel that carries it
- I can build a map of loss for my identity just by looking at the moon.

—∞—

On June 24th, every year, people in the western Carpathians of Romania celebrate *noaptea de Sânziene*, the *Sânziene* night, a holiday similar to the Swedish Midsummer celebration.

The name *Sânziana* comes from the Latin *Sancta Diana*, Saint

Diana, the Roman goddess of the moon, countryside, hunters, and the forest, also celebrated in Roman *Dacia* (the ancient *România*); the virgin goddess, protector of women and maidens, one of the 3 goddesses who swore never to marry.

On June 24th, as tradition imposes, the most beautiful maidens in the village dress in white and spend all day searching for and picking flowers, of which one MUST be the yellow *Galium verum* (lady's bedstraw or yellow bedstraw), also called *sânziană* in Romanian.

Sancta Diana, the virgin goddess, one of 3, daughter of Jupiter, Father of the Sky.

—~—

When I am 8 or 9, my visual artist and scientist father teaches me how to look at the sky. We trace constellations on the night sky in our search for meaning, for patterns. *Carul mic. Carul mare.*

I remember our walks in the park around the same time, him telling me that bats can get stuck in your hair at night. Yet at Lake Secu, it isn't bats we see, but fireflies. I remember them dancing in the dark, little flickers of tomorrow. I remember feeling safe.

I never learn to properly watch the night sky in my father's structured manner. I just look and take it all in.

—~—

In my childhood, I am afraid of heights, of climbing trees, of climbing the roof of the garage at Alina's grandmother. I do both because she really wants me to and I want her to keep playing with me. Who knew I'd one day put hiking above everything else. It is almost never the highs that scare me. It is the lows.

—~—

When I fall and injur myself, *mama* kisses the wound and says: "By the time you get married, it will long have passed." (RO *Până te măriți, trece.*)

But there are also other times, when she says: "By the time you get married, a lot of water will have flown down the river Bega." (RO *Până te măriți, va curge multă apă pe Bega.*)

But then I say: "*Mama*, I won't wait for as long as you have to become a mother. I won't end up having children in my mid 30s, I will get married and have children in my early 20s, that's for sure." And whenever we fight and she is mad at me, she says: "Well, I hope you'll one day have a daughter just as stubborn as you are, so that you finally see what *that* is like!"

On paper, I draw variations of a granddaughter, mother, and grandmother, and mark their ages: they are 18, 36, and 54 years old. It is what I have heard, that when you are 18 you are an adult and it is OK to have children. And I don't understand why isn't everyone just sticking to this rule. It would just make things so much easier.

Somehow, none of it happens. Neither the marriage, nor the daughter. And the river Bega, you may ask? It just keeps on flowing. And the wound? It remains unattended. And the mother?

—∾—

The mother lies in bed and can only move, or even sit, if lifted by others, while I am out, a thousand kilometers away, hiking in the woods, in the mountains, one step after the next, always higher, always farther away.

—∾—

Tata always wants me to have straight As in school, like he once did. Top of his classroom, top of his highschool. *Valedictorian*. Something like that. But *mama* says: "I will love you anyway, I don't care what grades you get."

—~—

My mother never had very big professional ambitions like my father. All she wanted was to have a husband and a daughter.

I am that daughter. Probably not the one she envisioned. One that always rebels against everything she stands for: against marriage, against family, against tradition.

"Where did you see people do that?" she would often ask me throughout my younger years abroad, when I would come visit my parents once or twice a year and spread my mess around my room. She would come by to chat and end up picking up my clothes from the armchair and start folding them, which always drove me half-mad. My father would come and ask her: "Why are you doing that again, you know she hates it when do you do that?"

In my childhood, when my parents fight, I tell my mother: "Shut up and do what *Cipri* says, he is the boss of our family!"

My father, when he gets angry (and that happens often), says: "I will put on my coat and leave!"

But he doesn't. He just makes a scary face, his eyes get very large and his thick eyebrows go up, but he never ever really leaves. Yet I always fear that he will.

—~—

At my grandmother's place, as a child, I love playing with the old wooden nested dolls. There is a big one that covers all of them, and then, layer after layer, there are more dolls to unravel. They get smaller and smaller and all look the same, except for their size. You can only get to the smallest once you've removed the rest.

They're both a shelter and a prison. Like a story within a story within a story.

Getting to the smallest one at the center is always like a little victory for 5-year-old me. I love watching her break free from all the other dolls.

Years later, I understand that she isn't really free. She is a wooden doll, either laying passively on the floor, unable to move by herself, or standing still, captive in my child hands.

Years later, I learn about ovaries and *ovule*. My grandmother's ovary already had all the *ovule* she would ever have throughout her lifetime when she was born. One of those *ovule* turned into my mother. And one of my mother's *ovule* turned into me.

For a long time, my mother tries and tries, especially after her miscarriage. Both she and my aunt have a fibrous uterus. One that would rather grow fibroids instead of babies. Later, this would also happen to me. My aunt has hers removed after giving birth to my cousin. My mother keeps hers after her misscariage and one day she's finally pregnant with me.

I reach puberty as my mother reaches her early menopause and her first of many long years of severe depression. Like there isn't enough room for both of us.

My mother's and grandmother's stories are heavy with guilt and regret. We don't talk much about them, but, as I get older, I start feeling their weight.

One day, in the fall of 2019, I finally get diagnosed with polycystic ovary syndrome (PCOS) and associated insulin resistance (IR). As my mother and grandmother never have, but should've been as well. So many things in my life, so many health struggles, finally start to make sense. I read that insulin resistance also occurs in the brain. It creates brain fog, anger, and depression.

I get put on metformin and a low-carb diet, which will last throughout my life, as PCOS never really goes away. One in 10 women have it and most cases are linked to insulin resistance.

I do not have any of the side effects that makes metformin intolerable in most people. After having worked for many years in clinical research, and in the first 4.5 years in that field, in diabetes research, I read a lot about metformin (which we used to bash back then in search of new and more effective drugs) and its potential use for treating anxiety and depression. I do not know if it is the metformin, the change of diet, the relief of knowing "what's wrong with me" metabolically after years of seeing gastroenterologists and hepatologists in vain, all the emotional and transgenerational healing work I have been doing (or trying to do in the last years), or a combination of all, but I finally start feeling like myself, like I know how to negotiate with my body and mind, listen to my gut for a change. My mood stabilizes.

But there is one other thing: PCOS is also the most common cause of female infertility.

Is nature trying to remove my genes from the overall human pool? Am I the last nested doll?

—∾—

In late March 2020, here in Munich, Germany, where I now live, we are still allowed to go for walks alone in nature. If we keep our distance. The only people I talk to after Easter are my neighbors. Mostly I talk to their daughter, Lenea, a chatty 3-year old. Her family and I live next door from each other but do not talk much, mostly we just acknowledge each other.

Social distancing becomes part of our everyday vocabularies. In Munich every other person is single. My partner does not live with me and he is not my partner.

"If I get stopped by the police," he says, "I can always say you need help. That I'm bringing you toilette paper."

—∾—

My new pandemic habit becomes this: I walk into the forested area of one of the local parks on my own, in the early morning, while most people are still sleeping, after crossing a sunny meadow with a lake. This is protected land, marked by a sign asking everyone to tread carefully as this is a land of amphibians and birds, not of humans.

I wrote a story once, years ago, in the form of newspaper columns, about an old Italian town that gets invaded by bees. The town's main piazza gradually goes from being a place of old history and rich tourism into one of emptiness and stillness. Demons looking like angels take the place of humans in their sleep. It starts slowly, the decay, the emptiness, but then it quickly takes over. Bees are usually associated with fertility, honey, their positive effect on the environment. But not in my story. The city is left empty of people who turn into corpses while the devil bees take over. Christmas is coming, and so is a New Year's Eve without humans.

On the *Sânziene Night,* the girls braid floral crowns using the flowers they picked during the day and wear them when returning to the village at nightfall. There they meet with their beloved and dance around a bonfire. The crowns are thrown over the houses, and whenever the crown falls, it is said that someone will die in that house; if the crown stays on the roof of the house, then good harvest and wealth will be bestowed upon the owners. Jumping over the embers is done to bring purification and health.

In some areas of the Carpathians, villagers light a big wheel of hay from the ceremonial bonfire and push it down a hill, as a symbol for the setting sun.

During that night, the heavens are said to open up, making this the strongest night for magic spells, especially love spells. Plants harvested during this night are said to have tremendous magical powers.

It is not good to be a male and walk at night during the Eve of the *Sânziene Night,* as that is the time when the fairies dance in the air, blessing the crops and bestowing health on people. They do not like to be seen by males, and those who see them will be maimed, or the fairies will take their hearing/speech and make them mad.

—~—

Another friend's daughter is 11 and wants to know about sex. Not just how it is done, but also how it feels. My friend tells her: "It matters who you do it with. It is not the same thing, eating cake with your best friend or with whomever."

—~—

Back when I was a child, the sky was never blue. Not in my drawings of the sunset, at least. There was no sun, but there were many colors. I dreamt of caterpillars turning into butterflies, of mermaids and unicorns. Sometimes, I was one. In summer camp, years later, the boy and I didn't talk at night. We kissed and danced. *Purple Rain*. He kept growing against my thigh. His palms kept sweating against my back. In the morning, under the pine tree at the waterfalls, his hair smelt like firewood after the rain. In the afternoon, we went searching for the sun. We found it in an orchard, in the abandoned village at the bottom of the hill. In an old house's garden, apple trees still grew. I took a bite from an oversized apple that fell at my legs, then another one. I pushed some of it into his mouth. He choked, I laughed. I asked him if I was too much for him, then kissed him and told him I loved deserted places. He said it was a sign that something or someone had been taken away. A silver door turned into a wall. Didn't I know that reality was never an extension of our dreams? It rained that night. In the morning, I stood by myself again, in front of the old abandoned house. Inside the large puddle in front of my feet, beneath the morning sun, the indigo was lifted up by an orange cloud. The old wooden blinders went open and shut, open and shut, open and shut.

—~—

Astrocytes get their names from stars. Astrocytes don't just clean up neurons' garbage, they also tell them what to do. Astrocytes are like stars, this is where their name comes from. Astrocytes are linked by gap junctions, creating an electrically coupled (functional) syncytium. Because of this ability of astrocytes to communicate with their neighbors, changes in the activity of one astrocyte can have repercussions on the activities of others that are quite distant from the original astrocyte. Astrocytes are good neighbors.

—~—

Very often as I am growing up my father asks me to take care of my mother. My mother is frail, naive, and aloof. It didn't feel like that when I was a small child and her energy levels were on a high wave. She has been sick for over two thirds of my life. Her sickness isn't stable, it isn't easy to define. It is selfish and self-sustaining. I ask my father many times to divorce my mother, but he always says no, you are young, you have to put up with it, you do not understand how much I love her. He refuses to get her institutionalized. For years I keep hearing my mother say each day that life is meaningless, or, in other words: not worth living. For years, I keep testing new strategies to make her leave her bed, shower, eat, comb her hair. Most of them remain unsuccessful. Later in life, working in a research lab, I encountered similar frustrations. Things often go their way, not mine, despite careful planning and consideration.

I didn't want to take care of my mother when I was a teenager. I wanted her to take care of me or at least to just let me be. Yet, years later, I am still taking care of my mother. I am also taking care of my father. For the past 2 years, this is what I have mainly been doing with my life.

I often need to remember to take care of myself, too. I often only take care of myself last, not first. I need to remember that it is not my task to take care of the entire world to the point of exhaustion. I need to remember that we all inhabit different bodies and that mine too is a temple of its own.

When my father ended up in hospital again last year, more than once, my mother gave up – once again – and let me take care of everything, every single time I appeared in my home town, from hundreds of kilometers away. Her psychiatrist shrugged his shoulders.

Ever since watching her father die in a hospital, my mother hates hospitals. Ever since he was arrested, she hates mess. To this day, my mother is obsessed with order. With routine. She cannot handle changes.

And yet, I insist to remain: outspoken, messy, defiant.

At the trial of my grandfather, which was a mockery, the siblings of my grandfather did not show up. They had their own families to protect. They did not want to be associated with this family. My grandfather looked weak. When my mother saw her father weak and tripping, she wanted to run towards him, but the guard placed himself between them. She wasn't allowed to touch him or hug him.

They lost their house. It belonged to the state now. My grandmother had to work as an unqualified worker in a factory. She, the daughter of the village priest and wife of a lawyer, who had never worked a single day in her life. She spent days in rubber boots, her feet and legs deep in the dirty water. She had to divorce her husband, whom she dearly loved, so that her girls could go to school and study. Still, they had limited choices due to their "dirty, unhealthy political background." My aunt, the elder sister, had more restricted life choices than my mother. My grandmother made my mother study chemical engineering, which she hated. She would have preferred to become a writer, like my grandfather also tried to be.

For years, nobody knew who turned him in. The family decomposed. And when my grandfather was released from prison and returned to the only possible home, he had leukemia. Shortly after, he was dead. My grandmother couldn't – at that time – afford to get him the treatment he needed. Recently, my cousin – who now lives in

Sweden and is tracking down all the shattered parts of our family, in an attempt to rebuild the family tree – tracked down my grandfather's files. The man who turned him in was a friend of the family, a German engineer who made a living building wells. He and his wife moved to Germany shortly afterwards. This is where I now live, as well as my extended family. In the file, my grandmother – the very same who would at times call my grandfather selfish for speaking up, for not protecting his family – is described as having "a loose mouth." It seems she was "lucky" actually, lucky that it was not her who ended up in prison. Then again, back then, women rarely did. It was easier for the *Securitate* to leave them to struggle for survival without a man by their side, without an income for their families.

For years, I roamed the world. I studied science but now I make a living as a (medical) writer. I tried to escape my mother, but she still got me. I have various physiological deficiencies, all associated with tiredness and depression: vitamin D and iron deficiency, thyroid underfunction, and PCOS with insulin resistance. On most days I don't want to get out into the world. I would rather stay at home with a book in bed, but I feel like I can't. I am the main source of income for me, and one day also my parents and my half-sister from my father's side who has severe paranoid schizophrenia. Thus, I am not allowing myself financial risks and emotional freedom. I am however testing new strategies for getting closer to doing the kind of work that I truly love. For feeling less caged.

Yet everyone who knows me tells me: "I admire your energy." My mother says: "You are strong and can handle everything, you are not like me. I don't know when you became like this, so tough. So stubborn and outspoken, like your father."

But there are days when I'm like her. For years, I fell in love with men who suffered from depression. I tried to fix them. To fix all the things I could not fix in my mother. I stayed in relationships that were bad for me, that left me drained and empty. I stayed because my father stayed with my mother. Because leaving them would have made me feel like a terrible person. All these relationships ended whenever I showed my own first signs of need, of sadness, of attachment. "But you were so strong and positive and independent when I met you!"

I learned very early in my childhood that families are a burden and unreliable. My grandmother would at times blame my grandfather for what happened to the family. As a child, I often heard her say she wanted death to come, sooner rather than later if possible. I learned that some people will always run away from responsibility.

And now. I don't know where I stand on the topic family. I meet men who take off and leave their wives and children because they "no longer love" their wives. They seek adventure. The women can't, they need to take care of their children. We are always taking care of someone. There are many ways of parenting. I am scared of families and how our individuality gets lost in them. Of compromising. I am sick of men who are not willing to share home responsibilities.

Growing up I felt imprisoned with my parents from a certain age onwards. I didn't know where they ended and I began. In a way, we are still all mixed, the boundaries, still blurred. There are genes I cannot escape and need to accept as a part of me. I know that hating parts of us means hating myself. I know it. And yet, and yet.

I am still learning that families can be good. That they can be dependable. That I don't need to do everything on my own. But I don't have healthy role models when it comes to sharing tasks and responsibilities. In my family, all of us have either been all in or all out. I do not have healthy role models when it comes to asking for help without placing the full responsibility on someone else.

Now, I am learning to face my parents. I am learning to stay far away from them, despite all their issues, and take care of myself, first and foremost. I refuse to be called selfish. I refuse to let go of who I am and what I do to take care of my parents. My parents made the choice to get married, to stick together. My father chose to tell me that he does not want help in the house from a stranger. We fight over the phone, a week after he is once again released from hospital. I cry in anger. And then I choose myself. I have done my best. The rest is their choice.

Years after the nieces and nephews of my grandfather's siblings escaped communism to Germany, I am finally meeting them again, some for the first time. We can now openly talk about what happened years ago, with my grandfather, with their escape from communism, back then illegal, despite their half-German roots.

I almost accept that I cannot relive my parents' lives and make their choices. As irrational as they may appear, they are still their choices. My choices, as bad as they may seem to them, are and remain my own.

My father used to tell me this fable until some years ago. An eagle has two babies. He asks them: "What will you do when you grow up and I am old?" Baby 1 answers:

"I will take care of my children." The eagle is pleased.

Baby 2 answers: "I will take care of you." The eagle throws Baby 2 out of the nest.

I get it. Life is first of all about survival. Yet, my father stops telling this fable when he starts getting old, frail, and spending time in hospitals, mostly against his will.

Life in the big city gives us the illusion that we can always meet someone new, someone better. Moving around the globe makes almost all encounters look temporary, even the deepest, most intimate and meaningful ones. Drifting away from places where we only lived briefly can make us feel lost. I am tired of everyone searching for something better, bigger, different. Our bodies are temporary homes. And yet, and yet, I'd love to find a body that matches my own. I am still learning my definition of love and family, of responsibility that feels like intimacy and not like a burden. And I know that if I do choose to have children, if I can have children, I will put their well-being and health first, before that of my parents.

—w—

Men and water. I copy this fragment from a piece of paper that I had spilled water on, the writing is in ink. It is about men who are like rocks and men who are like water. I wish to fall in love with a man who is a rock, not the water that breaks it. The writing is wishful thinking and I know, while I write it, that it is a lie. That rocks are shaped by water and water is birth-giving and everywhere. Water is imagination, the subconscious, but we can drown in it at times. I'd drown. I still haven't learned how to swim. Not in the deep waters, at least.

—∾—

I wash the grains in 7 waters. Or so the story goes.

—∾—

A friend tells me once: "The kind of man you are looking for doesn't exist, stop daydreaming. The connection you are longing for doesn't exist. You can have it with a female friend, but not with a man."

She is married to her university sweetheart and about to give birth. Is she right?

I take tests online to figure out my attachment style. I go from anxious to anxious avoidant during the period I now call "my healing years"; the secure attachment style still remains a mere 20% of my overall attachment personality.

The anxious avoidants seem to be the most messed up of all styles. We both crave and fear both intimacy and space. The truth is I have never managed to feel free in a relationship. Which makes it easier to choose men who I know will go away, because there is no danger that they will smother me, neither with their love nor with their needs.

I learn this late, when most men I meet are at an age where they have already been through 1 or 2 divorces, already have 2 or 3 children, and do not want more.

A friend in her early 40s tells me, after her own failed attempts to get pregnant: "It may be for the best, at our age it is not so easy anyway, you may want a child, but you may not get it."

I try to think like this but it is not working. Part of me still dreams of the traditional nuclear family. Perhaps one with less predefined gender roles. But yes, I find myself still wanting a family. Despite everything I have been through. Despite living with PCOS and IR. Despite my logical brain and biological caveats, my body is still longing to birth and to mother.

—ʬ—

Lakes and forests is where I feel most at home. Large bodies of water, although I am not a good swimmer. Trees with hundreds of rings and history and roots that break through stone, lifting their crowns towards the sky, searching for the light, even in forests that barely get any sunshine, always searching for that light that will take them one step further. They will be there in one form or another even when we won't. We are a very small part of nature on this planet and at times its unwelcome temporary guests, but we keep forgetting this. Dolphins return to the channels of Venice. Or so the fake news story goes.

—ʬ—

Lacul Secu. I am 5 years old. There is *mâl* on its bottom, a lot of *mâl*. It is yucky. I feel like I am sinking although I am not. In the distance there is wood, sticking out of the water. Traces of old houses, of people's homes. An entire village drowned. I do not know if people escaped or if their bodies ended up rotting at the bottom of the lake.

But years later, in the middle of the corona pandemic outbreak, I read about it online. The lake is artificial, man-made, 7 km away from the town of Reșița. It was erected as an "accumulation lake" to ensure the town's water supply in the 60s and also protect it from flood. The 20 houses and the wooden village church had to be evacuated and drowned in water. The villagers and the priest moved to a neighboring village. The railroad that used to carry wood to the top of the nearby mountain was also drowned in water.

The lake became an attractive spot for tourists. People started coming here in summer to swim, fish, or sail. There is also a camping area. Some types of fish one could catch here include *crap, şalău, caraş* or *plătică*.

Locals say that the lake is cursed. Legend has it that when you go by boat above the drowned village, the waters of the lake suddenly become transparent, and from underneath the waves you can clearly see the old wooden church and the house of the forest ranger. Other locals say that there are marine monsters and giant snakes living inside this lake, who attack people.

Locals also say that the lake has been cursed after the Secu village was swallowed by the lake's water (the lake carries the same name as the drowned village). This is why almost every summer at least one person drowns in the lake. The lake, once full of water and the once cause of relocation, suffered from drought in 2012 after a hot summer. All its water was suddenly gone. Afterwards the authorities left it like this on purpose.

Medicine Lake in Alberta, Canada is not a real lake but a network of underground water that comes to the surface and then disappears according to season. Hundreds of years ago, the natives of the land thought of the lake as magic. Believed that it had healing powers. That's why they called it Medicine Lake. They waited for the water to return from underneath for the magic to happen again. Medicine Lake is

more a river than a lake. A fake lake that drowns itself but not really. It is more than the eyes can see. A source of life, running free underneath, like the subconscious.

—∿∿—

March 2020. In January I have my precancerous cervical cells removed, meet my current partner/not partner, and, 2 months later, 2 new fibroids appear. I find out about them because, in the midst of the corona panic, my womb won't stop bleeding. But it is not a bursted cyst or polyp. It is not a spontaneous miscarriage. I contemplate – with my doctor – the possibilities: estrogen blockers; inducing menopause; hysterectomy. "If the bleeding doesn't stop within the next week, you need to come again."

That weekend a partial lockdown begins in Bavaria.

More restrictions may soon come in the whole country. "We will be observing the population's behavior this weekend." I don't know how this will look: policemen dressed as policemen, stopping people on the street, questioning them; policemen dressed in civil clothes, pretending to mix in (this would be the Romanian secret police approach); policemen with guns (shooting people who disobey in China). Fines of up to 25,000 Euro may follow. And what is going to come next? If we cannot contain the virus?

I go to my gynecologist again and there are no fibroids.

One Sunday morning, after the only full night we spend together at my place, the condom breaks and my partner/not partner has a panic attack. I take the pill after against my will.

On Easter Sunday, he leaves me. He is not as invested as me, he says.

I meet a friend for a long nature walk and this is how my nature addiction is reignited.

—∿∿—

Kate Bush has an album called *50 words for snow*.

Snow can melt in your hand as if it were never there. It turns into water and then the water enters your skin if you don't let it go.

My mother is my horse in winter, it is how I call her, when we are out in the park next to our home with the sleigh and I ask her to keep running faster and faster, while she is pulling my growing weight on the sleigh, the weight of a child at first. I am small, but demanding.

In summer, when it is hot in our home town, my mother and I stop at the water fountain in the courtyard of the Mechanical Engineering Faculty after going to the swimming pool. She teaches me how to cool off the inside of my arms with cold water, and also how to place cold water around my temples. Like her father, my grandfather, taught her to do when she was a child.

I do this all my life throughout the hot summer months and always think of them when I do.

—~—

As a child, one of my favorite games is rubbing my closed eyes. In front of me, patterns emerge, in what seems to me like hundreds of colors. I never know what I am going to see next.

With my best friend, I watch the total solar eclipse when we are 11 or 12. We are on my parents' terrace, at home, and my best friend and I hadn't been that close lately. But we share this total light, this total darkness. We look through a lens meant to protect our eyes. It seems so improvised, like kids' play, but it works. We do not go blind as the adults have feared we would.

Years later, I give my old kaleidoscope to her daughter. She is only 5. "And a half," she'd proudly say. I teach her how to turn it around. "It's pretty," she says. "Now let's pretend that we are teenagers. I am 15, you are 18, and *mama* is 19." She seems happy with this arrangement. "And we all have long hair and boobs," she adds without hesitating.

One year later, she tells us both after we once again eat ice cream together: "You both have boobs and they're a bit too big." She shows us how to wear our bags sideways differently, so that our boobs look smaller.

—∞—

A lot can grow underneath the snow. A seed can wait for a very long time to grow, under the snow or after a fire.

—∞—

We are now like Edward Hopper's paintings. Individuals in empty indoor spaces, staying within uncomfortable distances from one another. In sealed houses, in different provinces, different countries, away from our families and friends. Remembering the sunshine on our skin. Life becomes a story we tell ourselves or others, when the evening comes, perhaps in front of a fireplace over a glass of wine, but never at the seashore, facing the horizon, not anymore. We hug the person who is next to us, if we are lucky enough to have one. United and divided by our pain. On some days, we open the windows and let the spring light in. While we still can.

—∞—

Particles in the wind. Airborne nanoparticles. I study such things during my postdoc in Canada. Droplets with a deadly virus. The ashes at Chernobyl. When everything explodes but also years later, when the forest catches and recatches fire. The breath of a whale filtered by a sunbeam, just above the water. The earthquake in Zagreb. Droplets entering your lungs. The neurons under the microscope, like a well-defined constellation. In search of each other. Building networks. Together apart. Tree roots and stars in the night sky. *Carul mic, carul mare.* Walking in the forest on Easter, after the break-up. Walking with friends, walking all alone. Strings of candida growing inside my vagina and potentially inside my gut. The eruption of a volcano. The legs that keep pounding on roads, one step after another, one step after another, one step after another. The snake in the grass, greener than grass, on the carpet of dead leaves, because it's not only in fall, but also in spring, that certain parts of the forest are filled with dead leaves.

—w—

In a writing workshop, a woman tells me: "Remember that grief stays in your lungs. They say, in Chinese medicine, that grief stays in your lungs for a very long time. Be careful, take care of your health."

—w—

Summer 2018. Pop-up hotel, the walls are tall, like the room where I grew up. It is a place that does not belong in this city. The city is posh, this place is alternative. Or so it feels at first glance. It is mostly an alternative place for non-posh rich people.

The first event I attend here is a poetry evening. With a friend (at least at that time we were something like friends). The place says: "Nobody belongs here more than you." It is a quote from Miranda July. It also says: "All places are temporary places." This place is called *The Lovelace,* like Amanda.

It is the only place where I feel like I belong in this city, because it is a space of non-belonging, a space that will vanish, soon, too soon.

I go here, I mean there, up on the terrace, and inhale the too hot summer air. Even at night it is too hot. I want to bring the man I am in love with here, but only manage to bring another man, a tourist, a Brazilian living in France. We talk. He wants to come to my place, but I don't let him.

I have short hair in these memories, it is when I try to annihilate my sexuality but keep failing at it. I just anihilate my feminity, but that does not prevent men from wanting to sleep with me without getting to know me, it does not prevent them from feeling entitled to asking for it, or to coming before I do.

But this has nothing to do with this place, it is just about a period in my life, of many starts, of many changes, of many endings.

Before my mother became fractured into bits and pieces of brain, once again, just like in my childhood, memories disconnected, scattered, without a sense of self or direction. Before I started writing about all this searching, this longing, for love, for belonging, but mostly for myself.

I had never seen a pop-up hotel before. But in a way, any place you will never visit again is a pop-up hotel in your mind. A hotel, a summer camp. A house that no longer feels like a safe home or a house where you are no longer welcome. "All places are temporary places."

Like the abandoned villages in Banat, where people left and did not lock their houses. They left because they could leave. All the German villages in the Romanian countryside. Abandoned, but there are still things inside those houses, inside those kitchens, that say that someone once lived and breathed and ate to survive and slept to rest there. Even when it snows, there is still furniture inside the once bedroom, inside the once kitchen. A lot of things can hide and grow underneath the snow, waiting for their time to emerge to the surface.

—~—

Traces of the bodies at Chernobyl are still in the air. Black dust. All the bitumen that melted and turned into black dust. Dust is not supposed to be black, it is not supposed to be radioactive. I read about Chernobyl. About the people who left and about the people who didn't leave. About the women who could not help themselves from hugging their husbands even though they were full of radiation, of the babies that kept growing in their bodies, but once they were born, didn't, couldn't live. Of the men who were buried deep underneath the ground, surrounded by things that no humans are usually surrounded by, as a state secret. As if they were war criminals. Mass murderers. I read of Chernobyl as a place of stories of individuals. Not as a place of abandonment. Not as a place of nuclear tourism. But their place has been taken by other bodies, of nonhuman creatures, creatures that now have room to grow. And in some of these villages there are new houses, people from the city, music festivals. Life grows wherever it can, it takes the shape of walls at times, and, at other times, of music.

—~—

Dust can make you blind if it is the wrong kind of dust. If your eyes get destroyed by it instead of your tear glands wiping it out in time. And to some people, being blind is like death. Except that it is not death. For my mother, blindness would be better than not walking. But for my father, there could be nothing worse than being blind, because he is a painter.

He gets cataract surgery on both eyes when he turns 80. So that he can see again, so that he can paint. Pieces of his eyes are replaced with new ones. Crystallines. "It may feel like a foreign body to your body," the doctors tell him. "Make sure to use artificial tears regularly," they say. Afterwards he must cover his eyes, protect them from daylight. Less than a year later, he develops glaucoma, in combination with his high blood pressure.

I have a friend who always needs to use artificial tears. She has an autoimmune disease that dries out her membranes. Sometimes the syndrome is secondary to arthritis. It has become so normal that, when we go out, she takes out her disinfectant and artificial tears along and pours them into their eyes. I do not ask her if her eyes are so dry that she could never cry on her own. Most people need the tears to come out of them, not into them.

—⁂—

When I am a child, my mother creates dust in our *sobă*. In the morning, she goes with a metal stick into the half-burnt carbon, while I am still half-asleep in the bed we share. It is in the depth of a Romanian communist winter that she does this. A winter that insists on repeating itself, colder each year. We also burn wood, which we buy in summer and store in the basement downstairs. Where *Tanti Berchi* with her rotten teeth used to live.

—⁂—

We now have video parties online, each of us at home, with our families or on our own, drinking wine and gin, eating nachos, practicing social distancing. Doing only the essential. In our video call, at our Friday night party, a mother talks about her 2 children. The girl tells the boy: "If you do not stop running around, and you get injured, and you die, your corpse will be shown in a museum, stuffed, like they do with dead animals." But the mother corrects her: "No, if you are human, that is not what happens after you die."

—⁂—

When we die we do not turn into dust. We are buried in coffins. I have never died before. But this is how it goes in Orthodox tradition.

At funerals, mostly you can see people's faces, their dead faces. Their eyes are closed by someone. Their bodies are washed by someone else. And if they killed themselves, the marks of the suicide are hidden, as well as possible. But sometimes it is not possible. It takes some time until we die for good.

A heart can beat on its own, even outside the human body. My mother's heart later beats unstoppably, until it breaks, but I do not know this yet. Her pulse always going up, up, up.

It is the brain that fights for life. It is the brain that is what we call will. It controls everything.

—~—

During the Chernobyl explosion, I was playing ball with my dad in the park near our home, the same park where he taught me how to ride a bike. It was a purrfect sunny day and we played for hours, all afternoon, while the atomic cloud was floating above us. I have no direct recollection of this, I just know it because he tells me about it, years later, when I am reading Svetlana Aleksejevic's book about Chernobyl.

What I do remember is that we were told, in classic communistic censorship style, to avoid spending time outside in the sun for some days after that. But it was spring and sunny so it was hard to stay inside. There was some talk of radiation.

But I don't remember anyone telling us not to eat vegetables from the soil. I don't remember any talk about hypothyroidism and thyroid cancer.

I am a giant for my age but very skinny. This changes throughout my teenage years. Later I get diagnosed with hypothyroidism. Later my aunt dies of brain cancer, still young. It starts as something that resembles osteoporosis at first, then she starts losing her mind, then they eventually find cancer in her lungs. By the time they find cancer in her lungs and brain, she is already almost dead.

—~—

Chemistry is one of my favorite subjects in school and later I choose to study it for my BSc. We learn about all the radioactive elements. I like the sound of Radon as it resembles my name, Radovan. One of my colleagues who is also called Diana comes from a part of Romania known to be radioactive, the Bihor area. She tells me that people in her region stay healthy as long as they live there, but start having health issues when they move. One guy she knows went to study in Cluj and when he would approach certain instruments they would start going wacko. Diana and I spend a lot of time together.

There are 3 of us in our class with this name. The third Diana will move to Germany, like me. A few years later, they will find her dead next to her baby and because she has no relatives in Germany, the state will incinerate her, as the cheapest option. I learn this from a common former colleague who lives nearby, but because she is not family, the officials do not tell her much, only that Diana died of natural causes. And her boy? I think about adopting him but realize I would not be able to raise him on my own. Not with my current work, parents, cats. Our common friend tells me about an old couple in another city who wants to adopt him, he is only 1-year old, but they are old, so the state may not agree. The woman used to know Diana and she cared deeply about her. I have lost track of this story. But for weeks after it happened, I thought about that child who will have no memory of his birth parents. Who will perhaps not be held much in life. What kind of life would he have? What kind of future chances, what identity?

Diana is neither my first former colleague to die before we turn 40, nor the last. A former high-school classmate commits suicide close to our 10-year reunion, by jumping from the top of a shopping center in our home town. They find notes that he wrote, strange things. He was an odd guy back in high-school. Always challenging our Romanian teacher, much more than I used to do. Then there is the old friend from primary school, who commits suicide in her late 30s, but I do not learn how. I do not go see her at the funeral home because I do not want to remember her like that, dead. I want to remember her laughing and full of life, even though I know now that most of her life was filled with depression. She studied psychology but never practiced. I last see her a few years before that, when she moves back to our home town after several years abroad. Back in school, in our pre-teen years, I envied her for her self-assurance, for her beauty. She always seemed so confident. She was always so popular, while I was the tall nerd. But I also remember my cousin telling me back then, when we were still kids, that any person, no matter how they may look or seem, even her, all of us, when we suffer we are alike. When we are lonely or angry or sad, we are the same. It is what makes us human.

—~—

It snows over the abandoned *Lindenfeld* village in *Banat,* and there is still furniture inside the bedroom, inside the kitchen. Even underneath the snow, life grows. From underneath the bed, from the drawers that no longer hold secrets worth discovering, of people with lives of their own, anchored in this place where human life no longer follows its old course. Life grows wherever it can, it takes the shape of walls at times, and at other times, of music. What if a girl would come to life to make music? What if the wolves decided this was their territory? Can wolves eat pickles left in cans more than 30 years ago? People would get married in that church and get buried in that cemetery. Now you can drive a tractor through the church, all the way to the field where farmers used to collect their crops. But nobody lives here anymore, not even the village priest, because what can a priest do without a congregation. *Lindenfeld* means field of limewood, of lindens. Lindens are hermaphroditic, having perfect flowers with both male and female parts, pollinated by insects. It is all that it is now, a field. If someone were to take a map and trace its history, they would find the people who once lived here spread all over the territory of contemporary Germany.

—~—

My parents and I used to walk a lot in my childhood. We would visit their friends and relatives and often on the way back home we'd pass by the old Observatory. I would ask them to lift me up. "Let's play bird," I'd say. They'd lift me up with their arms, my hands placed safely into theirs. It was dark and there were stars up in the sky back then. We never visited that observatory. Years later it is still functional, but I pass by it alone, on my way to the cemetery, several weeks after my mother's funeral. There are many chestnuts on the ground and inside the fenced garden the trees are growing wild around the old building. "They monitor earthquakes here," my father tells me.

—w—

Our forests are burning. The Amazon, Australia, Chernobyl (again and again), California, Oregon, Alaska, Siberia. In Croatia there is an earthquake. I remember the earthquakes of my childhood, with the books on shelves and inside the drawers above my bed falling over me while I was sleeping. I woke up covered in books.

—w—

My mother keeps family secrets inside the drawers that she can no longer reach herself. But I know they are there. And I am writing about them because I know this isn't where they belong. Each time I visit I would like to bring them into conversation but don't. They are there and I let them be there because I read each one of them and knowing that they are with her makes her feel safe. After she dies, my father and I search for them and for the money she has set aside for her funeral, but we cannot find either.

As a teenager, I would hide my writing in drawers thinking it was not worthy of light. Now I know better. I know the importance of censorship-free words and I know all about "the dream of a common language". These are stories that need to be told and embodied by disembodied voices and bodies. And if my mother can no longer tell them, I'll make them my own. I become my own mother, and sometimes, I am hers too. But I cannot linger in that role for too long. "The hardest thing ever is not to be anyone's mother," says Sheila Heiti.

—∾—

During the pandemic, I shed my old identities like old skins, like the snake sheds its skin in the grass in the morning. I let go of things and stories that no longer serve me. I make room for a new self to grow and for a while, in doing so, all I have is a vast emptiness. Like a big and empty field covered in snow. And then I wait. For what, I don't know.

—∾—

I keep trying to rescue people. If I stopped and invested all that into myself, I would never feel abandoned. It is easier to have projects that are not us. If only I invested all that into myself I would stop being made of fragments. But would I love myself more?

Jesus, in whom I don't believe as a biblical figure, asks on the cross: "Father, why have you abandoned me?" But we all leave someone behind, someone whose load is too heavy for us to carry. For me that is the load my mother asks me to carry each time: herself. The one my father refuses to share with those who could actually help him: physically caring for my mother.

And, what is worse, asks Kundera, the heaviness or the lightness? But then again, I don't know if he ever had to take care of his old sick parents. I doubt it. Or else he would never talk about lightness the way he does.

—∾—

I learn, during the pandemic, that being overly independent is a response to childhood trauma. The same thing for co-dependency, prioritizing other people's needs, attracting narcissistic partners, etc. It all adds up. Looking back, I feel like my parents' generation as well as my own (at least my generation in Romania) – we are all very co-dependent. I am a living, walking paradox: someone who is both too co-dependent and too independent to fit in.

—ɯ—

We abandon our dreams for the sake of money and apparent security. We abandon.

—ɯ—

A man I used to love sends me a postcard. He no longer lives in the town of Ulm where we first met, and both of us live in a country where we were not born, Germany. The postcard is old and ugly. There are buildings on it that mean nothing to me and everything to him, because they are from his old town, a North American city in the middle of a flat nowhere. It is he who first talks to me about places being marked, defined even, by absences.

"...20 years

Absent are all of the city's most recent and iconic structures, the things we've come to believe are what makes this city what it is. And yet, here they are, absent. I find it bears a certain charm, like old photos of parents with funny haircuts + queasy sweaters.

Mere hours remain before I depart this frozen landscape. I'm going to miss it, much more than I did leaving it originally. If life is about discovering ourselves, then I've lived a lot these past few weeks.

I hope you enjoy this awfully vintage post-card. It has been adorning the postcard rack of my parents' small shop for the better part of the past...

Yours most nostalgically..."

He also sends me a postcard from Prague, from the Pablo Picasso museum, a city we both declare to be our favorite in Europe. It depicts a black-and-white reinterpretation of Velazquez's *Las Meninas* (*The Girls*). A city where he would live years later.

"Liebe Diana,

as much as I loved Barcelona, I have to say, Prague is kind of overwhelming. It's almost too beautiful...

I feel like I could just stay here forever, haunting its parks and cafés, reading books, and assembling a page or two of my own crude machinations..."

His favorite book is *The Little Prince*.

Sometimes I feel like we see each other, like we are soulmates. The way we talk about art and books, the way we love words, the way we sometimes look at each other. The way he imagines my home town, my childhood dreams, and my teenage years of roaming my city and its bars that are never too far away from home.

I write him an email somewhere in between, where I tell him, with immense fear of his reaction, that I realize I do not crave marriage and giving birth to babies, or to be a supporter of my husband and children, but rather, how important it is to me to forge my own path, to follow my own voice and its own need to unfold. He then tells me on FB messenger, 2 weeks later, that he has started drafting an answer to my email, but hasn't finished it.

He will never finish that answer. He will, however, "find" himself "in a relationship with a great girl" (to quote him). I do not quite understand how that works – I never randomly "find myself" in relationships.

I find his postcards nested on top of each other only in 2021, after moving many times, each time wondering where they were; they had been hiding from daylight underneath the cover of Alice Munro's short story collection *Something I've Been Meaning to Tell You*.

I forget the content of that email for many years and keep making similar mistakes with men, bending my ways so that things work in a way I think relationships should. I forget it for many years, but in 2021, on the Spring Equinox, a day still filled with snow in my little Bavarian village where I moved before Christmas, I dig it up and there is only this sentence that made me cripple back then, worrying about the pain I'd cause him by simply writing it. I find it and include it here, to make sure that this time I won't forget it again:

"If I am being honest with myself, studying makes me happy, and I am not the settling down marrying type willing to support her husband profesionally while putting my own passions aside to accommodate his."

At the time I wrote that email, I was dreaming of living in an English-speaking country again and pursuing advanced degrees and ultimately academic teaching in Creative Writing.

You see, in 2014, the man is my age, maybe one year younger, but he is studying and he does not have money for anything, not even to pay for his *Semesterticket*. At some point before he met this other woman, I fantasized about paying for his studies, supporting him in his academic career and life. I wanted to walk his path with him and save him. At the cost of my own life.

He never asks for that explicitly, not in words, at least, but I clearly feel, while we are pseudo-dating, that he wants to *be mothered* more than he wants to *partner up*. Don't all men want to be mothered and served?

Less than 2 years later, this same man tells me he is no longer in a position to maintain our friendship. He seduces this woman-girl using the same strategy that he used on me. He cleans and cooks, all the things that I am not good at, despite being a woman. We are no longer in each other's lives and this is just the beginning.

I could leave out the part where, before he gets together with her, I tell him not to come visit me because I have a new boyfriend. I could leave out the part where he is once in this Ulm town of mine, which I have adopted as mine, but I am not in Ulm, because I am away, visiting my parents. He sends me a postcard from Ulm, saying it is weird he is there and I am not. A friend who knows him says: "Sure, he would have liked to screw you again." The man is allergic to cat hair, and, as we get closer, he becomes more and more allergic to my cats.

The man is an editor and I am a writer. He is one of the first people to see my draft texts. But then, he once tells me that women writers would make good whores. And here I was, thinking we shared an intellectual connection!

Often, I am the woman either before or after the wife; never the wife. It is hard to say how much of that is my own choice at times.

In many ways, love and friendship are not that different. Except that we do not have a language or rituals around a friend breakup. And every friend breakup seems to bring new challenges of its own. And then there are all the friends I haven't seen in decades, who now live in other countries than our own, in other places than the ones I chose to call home. But simply calling a place home doesn't make it one. I have friends who know this and, like me, regardless of where they are now, they know, I know, that we have more to share than ever; we have learned the hard way that we need to make our own minds and bodies our homes. And that the thoughts we feed our minds matter.

I am my own temple, this is where I pray. Everything I need is within me.

I do not have any other gods, except maybe language, except maybe nature, except maybe a longing that I cannot fill with anything other than words and legs and arms running free over fields of poppies. Or with a voice that makes the earth and the air tremble in recognition and belonging.

—∾—

Atmospheric testing of nuclear weapons between 1945 and 1980 ushered in the "atomic age" and released large quantities of anthropogenic radiogenic nuclides into the atmosphere. These radionuclides remained as fallout on the entire surface of our planet. While many have decayed to negligible levels, long-lived radionuclides still persist and will continue to do so for thousands of years to come.

—∾—

My father is born in the Banatian village *Sânmihaiu Român* at the start of WWII. His father, the village school teacher, suffers from tuberculosis. I only learn this in 2020. For many years, my father is not allowed to eat from the same plates or drink water from the same cups as his father. During this time, soldiers of different origins – Romanians, Russians, and Germans – keep seeking refuge in the basement of their home.

—∾—

The persistence of memory. Is it real or is it an illusion? How do we perceive time? My mother's brain is made of bits and pieces of memories in a very nonlinear time. Sometimes she thinks I am her sister. Sometimes she talks to her mother. She sees them in the kitchen. But it's not them who are there, it is my father who cooks.

"Your grandmother was working in the kitchen early this morning again, I really wanted to talk to her before she left, but I woke up too late," she tells me on the phone. She forgets she cannot walk. She wants to get up and do things. Laundry, among many other things.

I spend so much time in the past since I started writing this book. And everything in it is fragments. But at the same time, I know who I am better than ever before. I am no longer a child and I am no longer her mother, although she keeps trying to turn me into one. But I can't. I just can't do it anymore. However, I do think about my childhood with her, my father, my aunt, cousin, uncle, and grandmother more than ever before. Because for my parents, memories are all they have now. My mother's long-term memory is excellent, but she forgets what we talked about and agreed on doing just half an hour ago.

—᠁—

I write at a table with women from different countries. We are only 3, times being as they are. But we are not scattered all over the earth, instead we gathered here with a common intention: to work on our stories, all these different threads from the big universal story that is life and the human condition, all these threads that all flow into the same story eventually.

We tell stories to survive, to make life bearable. We tell the same stories all over again, but nobody has lived them like us before, in these bodies, in this time.

I remember this Romanian joke I read recently: "I decided to gather my thoughts. No thought came to the gathering."

But we are here. With presence and intention.

—᠁—

My friend who studied to become a psychiatrist but she herself was suspected over time of both schizophrenia and bipolar disorder tries to convince me to write a book together, about mapping the brain. She tells me how when she does not sleep, she starts thinking abstractly, in symbols. She tells me that she is full of energy, ideas, imagination, but cannot always regulate her emotions. During her last exam session she almost lost it again, her mother had to come and take her to a psychiatrist, who gave her a small dose of sleeping pills.

She tells me how she does not believe there is a single gene for schizophrenia. How smart people who end up in a psychiatric institution may never get out of there if they do not know how the system works, how they might get entangled. How she was very lucid while they thought she was being paranoid and very careful with what she might say, so that she wouldn't get stuck in-there. That the doctors do not care if she studies medicine or not, that they only see her as a patient when she tries to talk to them about her symptoms in medical terms. She tells me how she does not want to lose her access to her creativity, drive, ambition, and imagination.

A common friend who meets her through me is the first to ask me: "Is something wrong with her?"

"There is nothing wrong with her, she is just temperamental, we Romanian women are like that."

But then I don't know. She and I, we are alike. But when I am depleted she is full of energy. And because we engage in so many things, art, science, and (in her case) also sports, we almost never just hang out.

She gives me the book *The Gene* on my birthday before telling me all of this, but when she gives me this book she cannot really tell me her entire story or why giving me this book is so important to her. We go shopping instead.

—∾—

My parents and I travel a lot during summer vacations. At Herculane, in 1988, I am wearing a dress from a family friend living in Germany. On the dress, there are 3 little girls wearing hats and pretty dresses, looking at the sky. The little girls are looking at the moon and stars. The dress is dark blue and, to me, it looks like the sky.

—∾—

I look at the CT scan of my mother's brain that shows stars, white stars, which mean lesions. She has complex brain degeneration and the neurons that died can no longer talk to each other, but the ones around them can still be rescued. Or at least, their death can be slowed down, if not prevented. She gets shots with cerebrolysine every 3 months.

I think of the map of the brain. Whether we can really map everything. Whether we can really see what bipolar depression has done to my mother's brain. What paranoid schizophrenia has done to my sister's brain. What my (self-diagnosed occasional) anxiety and depression look like when I don't take metformin and insulin resistance is making fun of my brain. How much of that is my true identity? It is all invisible in my social me.

A neuron shrinks when it dies. All its connections are lost. It withdraws its many arms from possibility and its surface diminishes into a bright spot on a dark sky. There is nothing around it except the darkness.

I do not remember that specific time when I played ball in the park with my father, but I do remember other times with him in the park. I remember running to meet a little boy who was far away from us and in my excitement ended up with a foot deep into a mud puddle, crying for what seemed like forever at the shock of the cold dirty water soaking my shoe and sock. Or: we cross the street and I do not look if cars are coming. And there is a car coming so my dad yells and yells and I struggle with 2 shocks at once, both that of the car that almost hit me and of my father getting so angry. There are also many old photos of me at different ages running around or with puppies or kittens. It is a way of documenting our lives.

Nowadays it is possible to take photos all the time and anyone can do it. We take a lot of photos and almost never look at them again. I do it too, but in my case, it is mostly landscapes, and rarely images of myself, rarely selfies. They say we photograph that which we are afraid of one day losing.

When I visit my parents now, it is me who takes photos of my aging, shrinking father. He is soon to turn 81. Perhaps I will be able to visit my parents then, like I did last year on his birthday, when he had his second eye surgery. If the virus stops spreading. Perhaps I will be able to host my workshop at the conference supposed to take place a week before his 81st birthday.

I dig up old photos to prove to one of my nieces that we do know each other in person. In these photos, I am 12 and she is 3 or maybe 4. In one of them, it is her birthday and we are eating birthday cake. In another one, she is at our place, my parents' home, on the terrace. I am arranging her belt and she is wearing a jeans jumpsuit. (The hardest thing is not to be anyone's mother.) She has no recollection of these moments years later, but is happy to see the photos that my father took.

My relatives are spread around Germany and a few other countries. Few of us stayed in Romania. Most of us do not know each other. Some of us no longer speak proper Romanian or never learned it well to begin with.

The borders have been open for those who dared for quite some time. And even when they were closed, some of us dared. We have the freedom to move now, but around us at times it feels like there is nothing but dark space. We are a bright spot in a vast darkness, except we do not know our brightness.

We have abandoned our old identity and social narrative like an old skin. But we couldn't shed, not fully. All the things we buried deep inside us are still there, asking to be brought to light, seen, shared. Asking to build connections through story.

Bright spots on a dark sky is what we are. Like the bats. Like our dying neurons. Because we cannot stop them from dying, all we can do is slow them down.

We go on seeking love. We live around it, pretending to be just fine, but we aren't. And I am not talking about self-love, but about love from somebody else. Someone to validate us and tell us that we are actually alright, that it is OK to stop for a second and just be.

—∾—

At my aunt's funeral, my mother's sister, the one that my mother sleeps through, a child has an epileptic attack.

—∾—

We do not think that often about animals and the diseases they carry. I used to think about that more often back when I had cats. Sometimes, it is a disease that binds or separates us from one another.

I watch photos of people wearing large plastic bottles and other recipients over their masks, over their heads. "I do not want to connect with you," they seem to say. They travel like this to new places where they do not want to touch strangers, doors, toilette seats.

Book fairs are cancelled, but some are still taking place. I do not know if I should visit the Leipziger Buchmesse. Or should I just withdraw in the mountains? Where bats fly freely at night.

I read that the virus started in a bat, then traveled into pangolins, before making its way into humans.

When I was little, my dad used to tell me that bats could get stuck in your hair with their claws. This image haunted most of my childhood but I never saw it happen.

In the park of my childhood, where we played ball so beautifully all afternoon during the Chernobyl explosion, we would often watch bats fly high above the trees after dark.

I hate how bats are associated with vampirism and Count Dracula. I hate how Count Dracula is associated with Vlad the Impaler. I've heard about the vampire bat, but most bats aren't like vampires at all. They are like mice who can fly and have amazing hearing ability.

Flying is not something I could do as a hobby. I know people who fly. And even teach flying.

Due to pandemic panic, my business trip to Brussels is cancelled and people buy food like crazy, they stockpile. Saturday afternoons it is becoming impossible to find fresh fruit and vegetables. People have bought a lot of tuna cans, face masks, and hand sanitizers.

Fifty years from now, future generations will talk about it as we now talk about the Spanish flu. This virus affects mostly the eldery and immunocompromised people. The Spanish flu affected mostly healthy adults, because they had the strongest immune response to it, and in the end that is what killed them. They were coping with it "too well".

We spread HPV through sexual intercourse. And it can cause cancer. But we do not seem to care. We just go on having sex as if nothing can happen. Most men aren't even aware that they can pass it on, that they're carriers.

In Germany boys and girls in their pre-teen years get vaccinated as part of the national healthcare plan. In Romania and Portugal, it is only girls.

I had HPV16 and precancerous cervical cells. I am now paying for my own vaccines. Nine human papilloma virus (HPV) strains that can cause cancer in one syringe, 3 times, 162 Euros/jab. Still better than cancer.

The standard of care varies from country to country. I talk a lot about this with a friend who chooses to have conization (cervical precancer cell removal surgery) in her country of birth, Italy. I am tired of having doctors poking at my body, putting me to sleep. And I hope that this is the last one of my so far 4 gynecological surgeries. And that my next "surgery" will be giving birth.

After *Konisation,* I have a high risk of spontaneous abortion in case of a pregnancy. As a PCOS patient, I have low fertility. Given my family history, I have a high risk of genetically transmitted mental health issues. At my age, I have a high risk of having a baby with other genetic disorders. With my new partner's age, we have a high risk of producing a monster child. But he does not want a child, so I guess that *solves* it. At least for the time being.

Paranoia around the spread of a virus. I am pissed off because there are so many other things that seem more contagious or more dangerous in some way. Fear travels faster than information. A man on TV says: "We lived through Chernobyl and there wasn't that much panic then. We were afraid of the water, of rain, of snow, of the wind, who knew what it may carry." Black ashes, star dust, memories of a time we wanted gone. Radiation.

There are days like this when nothing seems to make sense, add up, make me want to get out of bed. There are days when everything is silent and people live in sealed boxes that they call homes. There are days when your hand and my hand don't meet and everything worth living for seems completely out of reach. There are days and then there are nights when bats fly into the hairs of the universe and get entangled there.

—ᴥ—

When my mother gets home tired from work, I want her to tell me stories. All of her stories start with: "Once, there was a girl..." but then she immediately falls asleep. This is how my father ends up telling me stories, he paints them for me at night with his words. And I am allowed to change them as he makes them up. Instead of *Little Red Riding Hood,* we use all sorts of colors and all the girls go on different adventures, not just the one with the wolf.

—ᴥ—

Throughout my childhood, I play mother, doctor, teacher. All forms of caretaker. One day I drop Gabi, Laura's little sister, on her head, while running with her in my arms to protect her from an imagined bad person. We all feel guilty, but we do not tell anyone about it and keep on playing the same games each time we meet.

It takes me a long time to not feel shy enough to greet people on my grandmother's street, but once I do, I greet everyone. When my mother walks me home, we stop and talk to all the neighbors.

At night, my father tells me about that special flower growing on my grandmother's street, *Regina Nopţii (lat. Nicotiana Alata)* – the Queen of the Night. Unlike other plants, it blooms only at night.

—ɯ—

I will not write about the times I was attacked as a teenager by grown-up men I both knew and didn't know. On the street, including the street where I grew up, but also in what was supposed to be the safe space of their home. I will let you fill in the gaps. I will not write about it because it was common. One of them dates my friend and 1 year later, when they break up, we run into each other on the street and he tells me (forgetting the harassment): "Now we can finally be together." I cannot report the attempted rape because it is not rape after all (he changes his mind last minute and fucks my friend, his actual girlfriend, instead) and because his brother-in-law is a policeman. He is a security guard. I will not tell you more except that once, another time, I go home and wash my hands of sperm, then go to bed as if nothing has happened. I never see that man again but know he too is a security officer at a famous research institute. This happens again and again and each time it is not rape, because there is no penetration, but the penetration is always on the horizon, and I cannot choose to leave. I will not tell you anything else about this except that I was only a teenager.

Or: men in long jackets and on bikes who would stop me and my mother in my childhood, or only me later in life, to show us how naked they were underneath: "Come here with those lips and suck it," they'd say.

Or: the 2 Romanian young men on the bus in Dortmund on the way to the airport, thinking I didn't understand what they were saying about me in Romanian: "This one has lips that are good for the hammer." The 3 Romanian men on the train from Biberach to Ulm, my daily commute for 3 years, talking about my breasts and what they'd do to me if they caught me. I do not flinch. I let them speak. But deep down I am trembling. The many, many, many men, in Munich and elsewhere, who comment on my lips and breasts when I pass by, as if I were a toy for them to freely pass around once one of them gets bored of it.

And why would I tell you about all these things in detail, when they are day-to day-reality, so after a while they simply become normalized.

And then there is another man. A man I lose myself into and whose acknowldegment and attention I go on seeking. A man who always wants to meet, talk, play music, paint, cook, and do all things except one. He never touches me. When I touch him, once, he simply grabs my shoulders and pushes me away in disgust. And yet, for many years, I keep trying. Then, one day, I stop.

—~—

Memory, time, and imagination – moments overlap, like water, present is past. Like in *Slaugtherhouse Five,* there is sometimes an eternal present. The sky becomes a tapestry of our shared cosmic ancestry. Stars need to die for us to see their light. There are bright spots on my mother's brain scan where the light went out.

—~—

Our national poet back in Romania, the romantic poet Mihai Eminescu, writes a poem called *The Morning Star.* In it, the immortal Lucifer falls in love with a mortal and wants to become human for her, but she essentially cheats on him. This goes on and on for 100 stanzas. It is supposed to be a poem about the human condition vs. that of the creative genius. Our Romanian teacher in high-school adores this poem and everything Mihai Eminescu, a romantic, melancholic poet, wrote. Her eyes tear up when she talks about him in class. I do not always romanticize his melancholia, but I do love what he writes about cosmogony, the Roman hunting goddess Diana, and nature in general. My love for nature largely comes from his poems. In his poems, Diana seeks solitude and fresh spring water while the entire forest comes to life and all forms of life seek to mate. All except her. But then again, she is a goddess and not really alive.

—∾—

When I'm still a student in Romania and we play "what if" in a small group in a mountain hut near the wild Danube, the Serbian shore visible on the other side, a male friend tells me I am (like) an interrupted threaded piece. "EN If Diana were an object, she'd be... Diana is an interrupted thread." RO *Diana e o țesătură întreruptă.*

—∾—

Everything seems to be connected by invisible threads. Life and death occur in cycles. Memory and forgetfulness are threads. Life and love are connection. Death and disease are isolation. Love is subjective memory but the brain is deceitful. We are dust and stardust all at once. We are here to transiently shine our light and call it love. Genetics are both a blessing and a curse. We are made of other people as much as we are made of ourselves – like the night sky. There are less fireflies roaming around the earth than there used to be.

—∾—

Nature survives by experimentation, by mutation. It is trial and error. Nature always aims to preserve itself. We, the biped creatures of this world, are all nested dolls in the womb of the universe. In the stardust of our visible and less visible universe. We are seeds of possibility, waiting to be born. Waiting to be carried away, into this vast world of ours, a world that both is and isn't entirely of our own making. A story within a story, a tiny, forgotten, unknown tale. A walnut waiting for someone to come and crack it open, to release the seed, so that we can finally exist outside of our solitary selves. So that we can spread our true wings into the summer light, the summer fire, the summer rain, the summer wind.

Poetry and Nature Brought Me Back to Myself

When the pandemic started, I was brushing up the proposal for this book. I was determined to make it happen, to finish the book and get it out, but after a few days, I got stuck. I could not focus on writing my memoir or anything around it. I could not focus on revising longer work. Life was changing and everything about it seemed too near. On Easter, I went through a breakup. Everything that seemed to anchor me was crumbling down.

It is then that I started writing and taking long walks in nature again. Not because I had a purpose, but out of inner necessity. Here in Munich we've had a soft lockdown; neighborhood walks/sport activities within our immediate vicinity were allowed even early on. In the midst of all the uncertainty, on my early morning walks in the gardens of the Nymphenburg Palace (a mixture of fountains, trimmed bushes, wild forest, and human-sized sculptures of Greek gods), my writing started pouring out of me as short lyrical essays and poetry.

For me, poetry is much more about feeling than about form. It is feeling condensed to its essence. It is the unexpressed emotion that we all feel but that often escapes language. Our world is fractured, but it was already fractured before the pandemic. Free-form poetry and hybrid forms are simply reflective of our times.

In late April, my mother's dementia was galloping, she was mixing past and present more often than before. Perhaps this was her own coping strategy with the current uncertainty. She was seeing me 10 or 20 years ago and my long-dead aunt and grandmother, and calling my name often. My parents live in Romania (which has had a much stricter lockdown than Germany to date), and once again, we found ourselves separated by borders that seemed impossible to cross, almost like in the old days of the Iron Curtain. For several days, I struggled with figuring out how to get there. My desperation was not sustainable. Exhausted by various unrealistic scenarios, I remembered what Liz Gilbert had recently said in a *School of Life* webinar on resilience "There's a time to fight back, and a time to surrender."

I surrendered and I wrote poetry. And the more poetry I wrote, the more poetry I wanted to read. I discovered and rediscovered the poetry of Mary Oliver, Joy Harjo, Adrienne Rich, and Carmen Boullosa. Nature, legends, and myths have always played an important role in my life and in my writing (because how could I possibly separate these 2 from each other and myself?), but the more I read, the more I wrote. The more I walked, first in parks, then in cemeteries, then in the mountains (once it was possible to do it again), the more I felt the rhythm of nature within me and in my writing.

There's a new dimension in my writing now, a wilderness I had only tapped into briefly and temporarily before, which is currently looking for an outlet, day after day. The only way is out. On sunny days, I am outside, chasing lakes and waterfalls on my own, making my way through lush forests. On rainy days, I am at home, reading and writing poetry. I video chat with my parents almost daily and when my mother asks me "When are you coming home?" I remind her what year it is and of the current lockdown. We found a way for her to see me, for real.

I feel like these times are an invitation to tap deeply into our collective subconscious and unearth everything that has been buried deep within us: the folklore, the trauma, the archetypes, our true identities that we have tried to ignore for too long in our attempts of being as we think we "should be", as we think society expects us to be. Our connection to nature is dormant in many ways. We trim our lawns and often climb mountains to prove ourselves and our strength, but without necessarily stopping to witness the birds sing their song, water just falling, the trees with their interconnected roots and branches, using everything they can to root and grow, even breaking through stone, the ladybug gently moving forward on the path, or clouds moving with the wind. Poetry and nature open us up when we truly pay attention. Social isolation is also an invitation to embrace our real nature in solitude, in nature.

We often try to take on identities that do not represent us, we criticize ourselves and others. We try to love within a certain frame, as we see other people trying to love each other. But we also just are and life has always been mostly uncertainty, now it is just more uncertainty than usual. We can't stop death or the passing of time. We can't forever shove down our dreams.

Nature heals and re-heals itself and, above all, it just is, without trying to be one thing or another. In writing and in life, I try to be and do the same. I don't always manage, but right now, all I can do is write short, condensed poetry. I want my words to live on the page, expressing something fundamental, from a place beyond language, about life and human nature. Nothing "more." I want my words to have a meaning simply because they exist, rather than the meaning I try to give them.

More than ever, we need words that connect us and help us make sense of the new world. Words that aren't reflective of an academic, polished way of being in the world, but rather words that connect us to our ancient, wild self; words that express our true nature. We live in a liminal time and space, when our old strategies of being in the world and, most importantly, of being with ourselves, are no longer working. Poetry itself is a liminal experience. Whether we read it or write it, it's a vessel that can carry us through if we allow it.

Voice IV – Iuliu

(Space; Water)

Iuliu in His Own Words

Rain

I watch the window,
The places where the resounding raindrops hit it
Disappearing...like a life
Into everyone's heaven...into the ground.

1956 - Excerpts from My Brother Ion's Life

Life is a garden and humans are gardeners. The will, the character and the temperament are the 3 factors that our happiness or unhappiness in life depends on. If we take a close look at the role played by each, we can easily conclude that each has a longer or shorter route based on whether their determinant factor – the human – knows or does not know to develop their purpose, or – more specifically – based on how well each gardener knows to nurture the flowers in the garden he or she is cultivating. As required by the circumstances, the gardener will graft flowers initially meant to perish and ensure that they turn into the most precious adornment of his garden, garden that can be discussed about in different ways, based on the degree of skill of those participating in the discussion.

—~—

Ion was an honest man who never tried to appear in
any other way than he was. Was Ion a free man?

—ꟿ—

The sun is so beautiful on some days, it spills its happiness with such intensity that you think you're dreaming and the reality of such a landscape isn't possible, except in dreams. It only takes a few moments for a dark cloud to completely erase the sun's splendor. For the rest of the day, the same sun won't manage to send even a single ray of light and warmth to those who need it. Ion died under similar circumstances, but the light on his face, his endless kindness have never reappeared. He was and is no longer...all we have left are his deeds, many of which are worthy of being told to those who did not know him. I am particularly addressing those family members who need to know that the fate and hurt of a human being should not be locked inside a human heart. The heart has the duty to ask for help. The heart has the duty to ask for advice under circumstances when the will and the temperament do not know how to fight for the removal of human villains, do not know how to win against the will and the temperament of the enemy, who instead of helping take advantage of a large soul, of a pure heart, step over it, and even go to the extent of destroying their owner, forcing the one under attack to give up his own heart, as my brother has done.

—ꟿ—

Life is the only school in which we
learn to tell truth apart from lies.

—ꟿ—

Ion pulled a knife through his heart, on Serbian New Year's Eve (14 January 1948) near the train tracks, after leaving his office. The coroner pointed out that among 10,000 suicide cases, there is 1 like Ion's. This seems to suggest that this act was not random and had one or more preceding phases. Weeks before that, Ion was saying that life had no purpose. The last time I talked to him, it was on the phone, and he was telling me how he misses discussing with me. This discussion never occurred. Ion died with a desire to escape life, which he fulfilled. I will often think of you, Ioane, just like you have always thought of me with honesty, each time your gentle face will reappear from the world you live and in which we will meet again.

—~—

In the dawn of the next day (15 January 1948), I got off at the train station in Timișoara and bought a newspaper, the only one available at that time (RO *Luptătorul Bănățean* – EN "The Banatian Fighter"). In this newspaper, I found a phrase from which it was clear that Ion committed suicide, without further comments.

"The suicide of the accountant Ioanovici
from the Financial Administration

Yesterday before lunch, Ioan Ioanovici, accountant at the Financial Administration, aged 50, committed suicide. The named one left his office during working hours, leaving his coat and hat there, and went into the field behind *Manutanței,* where he ended the thread of his life by pushing a knife into his heart. The case is being investigated."

My Father Cristofor

I can still see him in front of me. I talk to him. I listen to his advice. An advice stronger than any other. His last minute advice. His rescue advice. One you couldn't walk away from even if you found a better one.

I had never thought of my father's death. Never thought that we would one day die.

The last Tuesday of his life, on a day when my soul was being tormented by restlessness, the phone rang. My brother-in-law, Leon, told me:

"Iuliu, go to Sânnicolau. Your father is in great pain."

I asked Leon no questions. I had no strength for it. I was convinced my father was dead. This strong emotion, perhaps unique in my life, didn't allow me to think. Cheți was at the train station, intending to travel to Sculea. I was afraid to pack black clothes, because they made me imagine my father's death. Over the phone, I asked the train station for my connections for the day. After a few minutes, they said I could take a freight train, the last slow train of the day had already left. I left the office and headed to the train station.

I kept trying to figure what was happening back home: agony or death. The first tears came spontaneously and I couldn't stop them. Perhaps my father's soul was whispering the secret of his cry to mine, and my reasoning was not prepared to understand it.

I was crying because I had to cry. I didn't want to meet anyone on the way to the Recaș train station, so that I could keep crying. My wish came true. The emotion I felt was so overwhelming that I wanted nobody around me. All my memories about my parents came running towards me from all the corners of their life. They were more alive than ever and together they placed the anchoring gentle face of my father in front of me, his wise but energetic look, typical of the whole man, who his whole life never hurt anyone, the look of the perfect man who never made mistakes, who only did good to his children and to any man who approached him.

A freight train took me, Cheți, and Dorina to Sânnicolau. In Timișoara we also met Leon, Feli, Lia, and Rodica. Ion and his son Coca were also there. His wife was missing, as always. Had father died or not? That was the question that everyone wanted answered. On the train we cried and did not talk. Ion was wearing black clothes and so was Feli. Leon was carrying black clothes in his suitcase. I was the only one with clothes that were inadequate to join Father on his last road. In the wagon where we sat, we were condoled by 2 men from Sânnicolau. One of them said that Sunday, 2 days ago, he saw my father taking a walk. His usual walks were, in his opinion, the strongest defense against death. Doctors had recommended him to take a lot of walks, and he respected that.

When we reached the Sânnicolau train station, Ion asked the postman, who had just arrived at the train station, if he knew what was going on at our house. He told Ion that Father had died. At the next train station we got off and, by chance, we were welcomed by the wife of Petru Paitity, who was the son of Doda Sofia.

In a few words he told us that when he had left Father's house, Father was still alive. Thus, my optimism had not betrayed me. We were all walking lost in thought. This time, getting close to my parents' house was the saddest return to this home, to the nest of my precious memories, a sadness that only death can separate one from.

My brother Gheorghe welcomed us at the gate and briefly told us what had happened to Father. On Tuesday morning, Mother had left the house to buy bread from the baker and thus Father stayed home alone. Next to the kitchen, there was a cement vessel that was meant to collect rain water. One day before, on Monday, because they had done a lot of washing, there was very little water left in the vessel. He bent down to get water. In doing so, he felt dizzy. Losing his consciousness, he fell into the vessel. Tuta, Leon's niece, who was walking down the street, saw Father fall and, with the help of their neigbours, lifted him up and sat him on some pillows. In his fight with death, Father won. The physically robust man with a strong desire to live fought to save himself.

Doctors Dad and David came in a hurry. They gave him a shot as relief for his pain. For additional support, a third doctor was called, Doctor Cristof, Father's permanent doctor since 1924, who disagreed with the shot administered before and gave him a morphine shot.

Father's fight with death terrified everyone who witnessed it. All of this was happening on Tuesday morning, June 19th 1945. At 8 pm, when I saw Father, he was still conscious. In order not to burden him, we went to see him one by one. He recognized us all. I don't know if he realized that just hours ago he had been fighting death. What I remember is his look, in which all the pain that one person can endure in the most tragic moment of his life was reflected. His look was lost, somewhere far, far away.

I took his warm hand into mine and the blood in me was running like crazy. Through his hand, Father sent me all his pain, his fear of death, and probably the most conscient hand shake, knowing that it is, if not the last one, then the nearest one to the last one.

Mother, poor Mother was running around like in her youth after the medicine bottle, after a caress, and, what was even more painful, she placed a candlestick, a candle, and a match box on the table near the oven. On another table, I found a small book, a prayer book older than me, which had always been in our home.

Night was approaching. A summer night without noise. Father was fighting in torments that only he could understand, we were not able to. And in his fight with death he kept his wholesome man attitude, it was as if only he alone knew that he would die and still had something to tell us. But he had nothing left to say to any of us. When the pain would take over he would say: "I cannot do this anymore... what can I do!" He could see for himself that we could not help him because we were helpless before the power of God.

Mother did not feel tiredness anymore. To save Father, she would have done anything, but in those moments nobody could do a thing. The next day, Doctor Cristof came, investigated Father, and prescribed him medicine. Poor Father took the medicine rigurously, with a single goal, to save the life he had built like a skilled architect. Many of his friends came to see him one last time and he thanked each of them for visiting him. He recognized them all. But I could not understand one thing. Why didn't he tell Mother or any of us, his children, anything about how to part with this life. An advice at least, on how he wanted us to honor at least his name, if not his giant work that he never mentioned. One thing he could not hide: the longing to live forever. A longing that many people lose in their 30s. It would have been in vain for him to express this longing in words, he expressed it much better through trying to feel better minute by minute.

Thursday came. The only day that he tried to get out of bed and sit in his rocking chair, where he used to sit and listen to the music on the radio. He also asked us to take him to the courtyard, probably so that he could say goodbye to all the memories that bound him to it. How much tragedy his soul must have endured, seeing it for the last time, and seeing us.

We returned to the bedroom. Around 4 am in the morning, while we were watching him, a choir of birds sang a charming song and with so much skill that it felt as if they were only singing for Father. They chirped for a very long time. It was the crack of dawn. Life was reawakening from sleep. Only Father was laying on his deathbed. But even now, I was optimistic. I didn't think we'd lose him. Then the bird chirping stopped. Father slept. I cried. I don't know if I cried as I am crying now but I know that I cried.

Close to midnight, Friday to Saturday, a dog barked under the bedroom window where father lay dying. The dog barked long and without interruption. When I opened the window, the dog took off. I can still see it now. A black dog walking peacefully in the middle of the road towards Rahaianu's house, probably satisfied that he had accomplished a mission that we interpreted as the announcement of Father's death.

On Saturday morning we asked Doctor Cristof to inform us about the state of Father's disease. He compared the body with a machine whose pieces had been used too much. In other words, he explained that he had done everything he could. The last of the honest aquaintances that came to visit Father was Cărpinișan, who ran the pub near the United Church of Sânnicolau.

This man's tears impressed me, he was an old man who understood the pain that Father was fighting against and who lived this phase of life that was separating us from death intensely. Father noticed his tears and acted as if he had not understood. Why? Because even now he did not want to let others know of his inner pain. It belonged to him and only to him. This supreme conception about the way one had to present himself in front of others, a way of perfect stability and continuity from birth to death is what we can call a wholesome man. How many of us would like to have such an attitude but can't? How many of us would have liked to be like my father in life?

In the evening, around 9 pm, an unsettling agitation took over Father. Accelerated breath, heavy look, and restlessness. He said that Eva Vintan was passing down the street, Eva who had long been dead. He said that she was coming from the town hall and we should not let her in. His last words to me were: "Iuliu, this is the last stop."

Mother had fallen asleep in the bed next to his. She was tired because she had done the biggest of efforts to help Father, the same way as she had done in 50 years of marriage, during which they had never offended each other. Ion and Gheorghe helped me lift Father's head further up. Father suffered for over 3 hours, his legs and hands were starting to get cold, his strong look from a long time ago was getting weaker and weaker, all hints that this would be the last night we'd spend together.

Father tried to place his fingers over his forehead, shoulders, and stomach in a last Christian cross, but his hands no longer helped him. His forced respiration stopped twice, and the third time he no longer breathed. Father died. The clock was showing 00:30 and the calendar the day of June 24th, 1945. Life followed its way forward, but Father was dead.

I could have written a whole novel about this last chapter in the life and death of my father. Those of his grandchildren and great grandchildren who will read these lines will only appreciate them when they will witness the last moments in their own father's life.

I washed Father together with Mother, Feli, and Ion. Gheorghe dressed Father in his most elegant black clothes, his *frac*. A few hours later, we ordered his coffin, and at 5 am we informed the mason to open the crypt, so that Father could, the same day, sleep his eternal sleep next to those who had been dear to him in life and whom he had lost long ago.

We do not know and will never know what his last wish was, because he had never expressed it, neither at the end of, nor during his life.

The mystery that had surrounded him from the moment I started appreciating him until the last moment of his life remains the most sublime lesson of character, of thought attitude, of living, and of penetration of the endless depth that life had given birth to, which we mortals can, in turn, transmit to our children, if we want them to be more than we are.

Father died without any of us 4 children being an accomplisher like he had been. Many people came to see him on the *catafalc*, because many people had loved him. To immortalize her love, Mother placed a photograph in his coffin that pictured them on their wedding day. I don't know where she had kept it all her life. Her words when she said: "May he carry my happiness too." Inside our house, everything was in mourning. I kept asking myself why he had to die. And I knew the answer: because it was God's will.

I felt the true pain of our forever separation in the church where the mystery of God forced me to cry more than ever before. Dorina, little Dorina, Father's youngest granddaughter, was holding her hands on the coffin like a child who did not understand what it meant to lose a father who was wonderfully kind, whose sole goal in life was to bring happiness to those he had been a husband and father to. Everyone was crying: Dorina, Lia, Rodica, Tibi, Limpi, Radu, Feli, Gheorghe, Ion, Cheți, Magda, and Leon. But the most profound cry belonged to Mother. I have always liked the church in Sânnicolau, even when I was convinced that some of the priests there were men without character. The Doina Choir sang well and all the choristers were there. This presence was the most beautiful gratitude that the Romanians in Sânnicolau could offer Father.

From the church, there was only one way left, and there was no coming back. The buildings we passed by with my dear father were sad too. He had nothing left to say, but there were still so many things left to say. On the alley to the cemetery, on the last alley that we walked together, I still could not believe that he was dead. But destiny is destiny and God's sentence was for good. When we reached the cemetery, Father was lowered into the crypt where his parents and other relatives were also sleeping their forever sleep: his father Ioanovici Ioan, born in 1822, deceased in 1912; his mother Persida Zarici, born in 1831, deceased in 1871; Alexandru Ioanovici, deceased in 1839; Vasile Ioanovici, deceased on December 23rd 1823; Aurel Ioanovici, one of my brothers. Going back home with my poor mother, I lived (possibly just like her) the saddest day of my life. When we got home, Father was no longer with us. He was sleeping his forever sleep next to his father, grandmother, his child Aurel, and his mother who had left him when he was only 3 years old. In the house that had remained empty without him, all I saw was his look, that look that his kindness, tenderness, caress, and everything that could be most honest, human, and understanding were springing from. Father was no longer among us, but we would always talk about him.

Iuliu through Mia's Eyes

MY FATHER FINISHED his high-school studies in Lugoj, in 1926. In 1956, 30 years later, he visited it again. His former classmates still called him Jabra, like back in the earlier days. He was a very friendly man, who liked philosophy, literature, and football. Since 1923, he had been writing, especially poetry.

When he was taken away behind bars, the chain of life broke for us. Out of 4 units, only 3 remained. The power was mocking the Eastern European intellectuals, who were uncomfortable people. They had ideas of their own.

At the trial, after hours of waiting, he was finally there, in front of our eyes. In striped clothes, his hair shorter, a thinner man, his body taking less space than before. He still had his dignity. He defended himself. But it was of no use.

The communistic system should be analyzed by the youngsters nowadays (1994) not only through the lens of the 1989 moment, but looking much deeper into history.

Iuliu's Oppressors

Where Do They Gather?

When the descendants of my grandfather's persecutors and oppressors gather to dine with what is left of their families in their solemn dining rooms with their aunts and cousins, do the portraits of their grandparents also reign over the dining table? Are their grandparents still alive? Are they rich? How many have made it out alive, when the big shots were called out and sent to court in the early 90s? What kind of stories are they told about their grandfathers? How many of their mothers have bipolar depression, believe at times that they are still under surveillance, to the point where they won't even talk to their therapist, because they trust no one? How many of their family members have undiagnosed PTSD and premature brain degeneration? How many of their aunts have died of metastatic brain cancer in their late 50s, and the last thing they told their nieces while still lucid was: "All my life I gave to others, cared for others, completed others, but nobody has ever done the same for me." and "You have a very heavy genetic background. Don't have children!"? Whose voice have they inherited? How proud does it make them to carry the voice of the oppressor forward? Do they only care about power, like their grandfathers did? How many mansions do they own, how many fancy cars, how much land that should belong to others but belongs to them? What kind of files do they dig into to find out more about who their grandparents once were? About their grandfathers, nothing was written down during all those decades of communism, because they were not the ones under constant surveillance. They were not "the class enemy." They were not the ones getting punished for listening to Radio Free Europe.

An Acre of Land

Before collectivization, my grandparents owned a house, acres of forest, and land, many acres of land. The day my grandfather was arrested, they took away all the money they could find in the house, to the very last penny. His ID. His free choice. His dignity. Then, they directed a mock trial. And another one. In the coming years, they starved him; beat him; broke his spleen. Broke him, us.

Memorialul Durerii

It's the early 90s. With my parents I watch *Memorialul Durerii (The Memorial of Pain)*, *La Piovra,* and *Twin Peaks.* Movies and documentaries aren't yet labeled with age tags. We sit together and watch it all.

Memorialul Durerii is about 4 decades of Romanian communism. Interviews with those who spent years in prison and labor camps. Survivors. We want to know how it was there. My grandfather did time both at the Gherla prison and at the Periprava labor camp.

He never talked about his time there; my grandfather who liked to write and share family stories, to help us understand our life better, neither wrote, nor said a single word about it.

After a couple of years, he was released and returned home for a short-lived happiness.

In her diary, my mother talks about him as a living corpse. She talks about how the *Securitate* (referred to as code name *Dracula*) ensured that her parents would formally divorce, to humiliate the family. She talks about the last time they went to the cinema together, he, my mother, and my aunt, to watch *The Great Expectations*. This is her last memory of them doing something together, outside the hospital where he eventually found his death.

And now we kind of know what went on in-there, after watching the series. Famine. Mold. Daily beatings.

We watch Petre Țuțea, the great thinker, say:

"I spent 13 years in prison for a nation of idiots."

On the TV screen, after many episodes, broadcasted in the late hours, my grandfather's name is listed, white letters on a black screen. In what should be a commemoration of the departed ones; of people, not names. He is one name of many, too many men who ended up being the great anonymous voices of their own history. His name is listed, but it is slightly modified, misspelled: *Iuliu Ivanovici* (the Serbian version of his name) instead of *Iuliu Ioanovici*. Once again, history has erased him from its records.

Or, as my mother puts it a few years later in her diary: "His name was modified through a letter, like the shaken shadow of a silhouette blown by the wind of forgetting. My father passed through life without making noise."

Later my father would describe my mother's death in similar words: "She ran out of air, her light went off, like the fire of a burning candle."

I also watch *Memorialul Durerii* in 2017, when I am older and alone in a foreign country that I keep trying to call home. When I decide that I must write this book.

The Records

It is 2011, just before I move to Germany for a second time. My grandmother has long been dead when we finally get a hold of my grandfather's security records. My cousin applied for them at CNSAS

(The National Council for the Study of the Securitate Archives) and it took 4 long years of waiting to get them. We make copies, read them, and then, as we tend to do with many other forms, store them in drawers at home. I remember my cousin, my parents, and myself, sitting on our terrace and talking about their content.

My cousin has to travel to Bucharest himself to pick them up, shortly before his immigration to Sweden. In these records, my grandmother is described as having a loose mouth. When the security agent pretending to be a family friend is sent over to my grandparents' place to make my grandfather express political opinions deemed "unfriendly" against the ruling (and only) political party, the agent is happy (according to the records) when he can talk to her alone, without my grandfather. She tells him things easily, perhaps too easily. My grandfather is described as being more suspicious and reserved. Yet it is him who gets arrested, not her. At the mock trial (for which my grandmother made an appeal, in vain), he is accused of:

- listening to Radio Free Europe (although their family was poor and thus they could not afford a radio except for a small one in the kitchen)
- having knowledge of and expressing his own views on international politics
- generally expressing a so-called "unfriendly attitude" towards the ruling party.

There are no further accusations, yet 605 pages are written about him, his friends, and family. In fact, he is so suspicious and reserved, that he is very careful both with what he writes in his diary (aware of the political dangers of his time) and with what he discusses openly, even with childhood friends, now security agents sent to pretend to want to buy his house, just to get him to discuss politics.

In the end, the main witness at his mock trial is a German water installation engineer, a so-called friend, who initially was the main target of the group investigation opened by the *Securitate*, the focus of which later turned towards my grandfather.

I will not include excerpts from these pages here; their repercussions are present enough throughout our lives and this book. Many of the pages written about him, some true, some not, are full of grammar and punctuation mistakes, as agents were not always educated people. The time in prison is not captured, except for one page, which remains partially blurred, and shows the atmosphere in prison and what the prisoners are doing in the words and bird's eye view of an agent.

What is obvious in these records is that my grandfather remains under investigation both before and after his time at Gherla and Periprava. A lot of the text in these 605 pages is either illegible or covered in black, anonymized.

In 2021 it finally becomes easier to obtain CNSAS files. It is possible to both request and receive information online, not just about family members, but about anyone.

Periprava

Periprava is a quiet little village at the Danube, in the remote Danube Delta, near the Black Sea, close to the border with Ukraine. The biggest delta of a Europe that turned its eyes away from the "Eastern Bloc" for decades. A serene place, at least at first glance.

From 1958 to 1963, a period of iron-hard Communist rule, the camp at Periprava held up to 2,000 political prisoners, including my grandfather. Many of them found their deaths here. Unlike many others, he didn't clinically die in this camp. They released him to die away, as he could no longer serve as laborer.

Decades later, on YouTube, I watch interviews with former political prisoners who have survived. Who, like him, were transferred from Gherla to Periprava and were "happy" at first, based on their statements, thinking they'd get more fresh air than at their former place of detention, so close to the Danube, to its Delta, to the Black Sea. Fast, very fast, everything changed. The undeclared and self-understood scope of their transfer was the brutal exploitation of their work. The goal was to exterminate them. The conditions at Periprava led to the death of at least 124 prisoners, of which 103 were registered. The youngest person to die was 19 and the oldest 71. Romania had about 500,000 political prisoners under communism, about one-fifth of whom died while in detention.

On the 25th of May 2015, the IICCMER (The Institute for Investigating the Crimes of Communism and the Memory of the Romanian Exile) started searching for and exhuming the corpses ("earthly leftovers") of the former political prisoners who died at the Periprava colony.

"It was an extermination camp," Andrei Muraru, Head of IICCMER, said of the Periprava prison in a hearing before the country's general prosecutor in 2013.

"It was a repressive, excessive, inhuman, and discretionary regime."

At the surface, before the exhumation work started, there were no signs to indicate the presence of graves. The place of the burials was found from local elders and former employees of the communist camp. The archeological investigations went on for 5 days. A total of 8 graves were found, and 5 were opened and researched. Institute investigators found skeletons of former prisoners who appeared to have been dumped naked into mass, unmarked graves.

—~—

As I learn from a Mediafax article by Marius Oprea, 2 days after my birthday in 2020, 12 days after my mother's death, 5 more dead bodies were found around a spring that went dry one day.

At Periprava there is a complex of shacks, surrounded by barb wire, which "hosted" hundreds of detainees. The detainees were supposed to cut reed, the main product in that area to be exported to other countries, including Germany. In addition, there were 4 ferries, or 4 floating prisons, if you will, which were permanently hosting a changing number of 1,000 to 2,000 detainees. Those who died were soon replaced by others. In the middle of this network was the central unit (hosting the commanders of the labor camp) and a complex of buildings that were also meant to serve them and their families, including a school for their children only, a heating central (oil-fueled, based on *păcură*), but also shacks for the common law detainees who served the administration.

Only the commanders' building has been preserved and is nowadays used as a luxurious guest house for foreigners passionate about ornitology. They are the innocent tourists who come here to enjoy the serene nature and beautiful birds of the Danube Delta without knowing, in lack of any memorial signs, anything about the human hell that used to take place here.

Overall, 124 people officially died at Periprava. A total of 50 (as found during the first 6 years of investigations at the site) were buried close to the earth surface, without any clothes on. Most were buried 60 to 80 cm into the ground; the deepest depth found for one body was 110 cm. Their bones were essentially left to lie in the sand. For a few, traces of wooden boxes made from hardened reed were found. Some of them had simply been wrapped in reed mats, surrounded by barb wire. Only a handful of them were placed in thin wooden boxes made from fir tree. Wood was a precious resource here, in the eastern side of the Chilia arm of the Danube. A 51st body (bones) had been stolen by the family of the dead detainee during communism, at night. A few falange were left behind. Most of the bodies had been buried within a square surface of 20 m^2.

In the 7th year of searching for dead bodies, 5 more bodies were found, close to what used to be a spring, now without any water, back then protected by wooden walls.

The locals told the investigators that they used to hear the squeak of the wagon at night and then the wagon dropping off the dead. The locals would turn off their lamps and move away from their windows to keep their families safe.

The spring was still full of water at that time. After the detainees were buried here, the spring started running dry. The locals stopped drinking the water from the spring and, from that time point onwards, used the remaining water only to water the flowers on the "graves" of the detainees.

Even official reports before 1968 show that "certain abuses were made in terms of alimentary and sanitary conditions."

After each exhuming activity here, the bones were carried to the legal department of the Tulcea hospital, then to the one in Bucharest, where DNA tests to determine the identity of the dead are planned, once money for such activities will be available.

Once money for such activities will be available.

I have to read this again and again.

Once money for such activities will be available.

I am "glad" my grandfather was sent home to die when he stopped being useful; I am glad that he did not die here. That is, if this can be seen as a small victory.

—~—

In the center is the old commanders' unit
Now
A guesthouse
For foreign tourists
A house but not a home
A house to watch birds for the foreigners
While others nearby
Dig for bones here, near the Danube, near the border.
The graves are many
And shallow

The graves are
Unattended
The spring ran dry
Feeding the dead bodies
Until
All that was left were bones
No
Wedding ring
No
Clothes
No
Nothing
No trace of the bodies ever being covered.
No mention of their names.
No money for DNA tests 50 years later.
No identities.
No no no
No memory
No recollection
No memorial.
Everything other than the commanders' unit
A ruin
Forgotten
Erased
Past becomes present
But nobody remembers.
Only this:
The screams at night,
Turn off your lights,
It is better to neither see nor hear.
A family steals a skeleton one time
But parts of its fingers are left behind.
My mother sells fountain water light-years away

While the spring where her father is imprisoned runs dry.
His traitor-friend is a well-digger, a water giver.
My grandfather's body is all parts, disassembled, broken,
But he does not die here, he dies in a hospital,
With a fake diagnosis.
His organs splintered.

—∾—

It is 2018 and in my new flat in Munich I am researching Periprava on the internet and looking at a photo of Ion Ficior, the former commander of the camp; in the photo, he is wearing thick glasses and a hat and is surrounded by journalists, after leaving the general prosecutor's office in Bucharest in October 2013. He was accused of crimes against humanity resulting in the deaths of 103 political prisoners from 1958 to 1963. The institute began to pursue Ion Ficior only 24 years after the fall of communism, when Ficior was already 85 years old. The institute spoke to 21 former prisoners to build its case against him. During Ficior's trial, former detainees accused him of beatings, depriving them of food and medicine, overworking them, refusing to heat their cells and forcing them to drink dirty water from the Danube, which led to widespread dysentery.

"Ficior beat us every day with a wooden stick," said former prisoner Ianos Mokar, adding that Ficior had terrorized inmates by "jumping over us on his white mare." Prosecutors placed a travel ban on Ficior because his son lived in the United States. I could not help thinking of the travel bans that had been placed on Romanians during communism.

Ion Ficior's arrest was shown on TV, just like the shooting of Nicolae Ceaușescu. In March 2017, Mr. Ficior started serving a 20-year sentence for crimes against humanity. He denied wrongdoing and said he had simply been following orders.

When my grandfather was arrested, they took everything of value they could find in the house, to the very last coin in the pocket of his trousers. They took his ID. Then there were clothes, everywhere. There were clothes, and he was gone.

I don't know what they took from Ficior's house when he was taken away. Did they take the house too? Did his wife go on living there alone? I don't know if they had children. Grandchildren. Great grandchildren. Did he use to beat and terrorize them too? The press releases I read only talk about other details from his life, from his much younger life.

Ion Ficior died on Wednesday, 26 Sep 2018. Bianca Filote, an IICCMER spokeswoman, confirmed his death at the Jilava prison hospital outside Bucharest. He died of old age, cared for in a hospital. Not of remorse. Not of the famine and beatings he had imposed on so many people who dared have a mind of their own. Nobody dies of remorse. I read about his death in the Romanian press, but also in a *New York Times Associated Press* article. This last release reads almost like an obituary, giving detailed information about who this man used to be. The information about the prisoners remain at best collective: 21 interviewed, 8 corpses found, 103 deaths documented. The individuals are not mentioned. Their identities remain those of political prisoners only. But Ion Ficior is given, in this article, many other identities: son of a Baptist couple, electrician, member of the Communist Party right after WWII, husband of Maria Căluțu, whose father was a Baptist pastor. After attending military training schools he became an investigator and bureau chief in the Romanian army's counterintelligence services. He was later transferred to the general directorate of prisons and labor camps and held posts at a number of camps before taking over at Periprava. My grandmother's father, too, was a priest (of the Orthodox church). That was before Communism, his priest days, when religion was still allowed in the open. When people didn't have to go into a forest at the edge of the town to pray. When Santa Claus (*Moș Crăciun*) didn't yet have to be called *Moș Gerilă*.

In an interview in June 2013, an unrepentant Ficior insisted that only 3 or 4 people had died under his command. He contended that his former prisoners were militiamen, known as Legionnaires, who had supported Nazi Germany during WWII and thus deserved to be incarcerated.

When my grandfather was released from prison and returned home, he had almost no social contacts. He was carrying the stigma of a former political prisoner and people kept away from him. Besides, he could no longer trust anyone. Not after 2 of his closest friends, with whom he used to exchange and debate ideas, turned out to be a security collaborator, sent to his home regularly to make him talk, and the other one a witness against him at his mock trial.

I feel like our family history, our well-being, our right to freedom, our right to speak up, all of these fundamental human rights were erased by history. There are numbers and dates and medical prescriptions. We are documented. But in the bigger scheme of things, it's as if so many things have been in vain. There cannot be justice done to so many families, so many generations, with one arrest. Thousands of arrests can't undo what has been done. We have to untangle the mess for ourselves, for our bodies, for our peace, for our children.

I haven't yet made it to Periprava. I do want to go, to see what is left of it. Looking at photos of the ruins of this place alone makes me cry. It is only layers of bricks now and grass that grows tall, well fed by the bodies of the nobodies of history. Bodies feeding the earth until all that is left is just bone.

In an interview, one of the few women who was imprisoned here together with her husband talks about their time in-here. A man who still lives in the village talks about how, as a little boy, he used to hear screams at night. After a while, he stopped asking his parents what it was. Asking questions was generally bad. It was better not to know. Or at least pretend not to.

It is important to witness and remember the pain. And then to feel it. And then to let it go.

Living close to Munich, I went to what used to be the Nazi concentration camp Dachau. While communists were openly anti-

Nazi, at least in ideology, they ultimately used similar methods to oppress people, those that they targeted as their "class enemies." Gherla is still a functional prison, to this day. It is a different story with Periprava. Like it was never meant to last, only to serve its short-lived short-term purpose. And then, to be forgotten. There is a large door at Dachau, and the words: "Arbeit macht frei." And trees with thick extended roots that grow both into and over the ground and look like human bones. The door makes the same loud squeaking sound when it is opened or closed. For most of history, it was closed. It is a place where people can feel horror and remember. There are many photos, explanations, things to read and see. Unlike at Dachau or many other former Nazi camps, the Communist camps aren't memorial places turned into museums. That people can visit, in horror, and remember. Periprava, like many camps of its kind, is a place that needs more witnesses.

From the photos I can see on the internet, showing what is left of the Periprava camp before and after the exhumation, there are no doors left, only ruins, skeletons, and grass. And a life that goes on in the village, in poverty and natural beauty, as if undisturbed by the past. Yet all former communist countries are aware of their past. My generation is aware of the trauma. Generations before us could not speak freely of their trauma. But my generation, we have learned to use this word to talk about what happened to us and generations before us.

The world outside still sees us as the "Eastern Bloc." But we don't. In each of these countries, there are people. People with unique individual and simultaneously universal stories that need to be remembered and voiced out loud. The story of communism is a universal oppression story. There is nothing Eastern about it. It could happen again anytime, anywhere. Because we still think of certain social groups as "the others." Because we still choose to turn our eyes away from the "other's" suffering. Because this awful selfishness and carelessness is also part of our human nature. We thrive when others fail. There will always be informers. Take away people's basic rights and start giving some of them privileges, and soon enough there will be enough supporters. This is how it starts. I am not talking about dystopian novels here. I am talking about our day-to-day reality. These days, there is a rise of both neonazi and neocommunism in Germany, the country that I now call home. Both terrify me. Oppression is never of a particular land or a particular system.

Iuliu through Diana's Eyes

Never

Like many political prisoners of his time, my grandfather had been accused of "troubling the existing social order through expressing an unfriendly attitude" against the ruling – and only – political party.

My grandfather never talked about his time in prison. He never recovered from leukemia. He was never quite the same.

A ghost around their old neighborhood, a trace of the man he used to be. He never worked as a notary again, never officially remarried my grandmother. Never got to see his daughters get married and have children of their own. Never opened up to anyone, ever again. Never trusted his neighbors. Never made friends again. Withdrawn (*retras*) is how the secret police files describe him after his time in prison, because the *Securitate* was still watching him, observing him, even after he was "released", sent home to die. My grandfather wrote, before being imprisoned. About his brother's suicide. About his father's death. About how he couldn't write it all down because it was too dangerous if some things would fall into the hands of the secret police and be interpreted and reinterpreted. He also wrote poetry but never published it.

He'd probably never thought he'd get out of prison "alive". But where can one go anyway when the whole country is a prison? When he could no longer trust his relatives, his friends, his neighbors?

He never got to hear my voice, hold my hand, know what it means to be loved by me, say certain things out loud, or travel outside the bars of his country.

I never thought I'd one day find my grandfather in a poem; that I'd one day be writing about him, about my mother, about us, about this chaos, about this fragmented puzzle that I get so lost in.

The Void

It isn't the void that
my grandfather is facing.
The void would be a blessing.
My grandfather whose voice
I'll never hear. It is the hours
of interrogation, the room
without a bathroom, the room
without a window, the room
within a room
within a room,
the four chambers of his own heart,
the longing for his wife and daughters.
But mostly the dirt,
the everyday dirt,
the hunger,
the cold in his cell.
The restrictions.
The need to confess and
not to confess.
There is nothing
to confess but they have
lists with
accusations. Beatings.
Blood. Silence. Yelling.
Alienation. A horse,
jumping. His blood count,
left unmeasured. A broken spleen.

The Cemetery

It is November 2018. In the cemetery in my home town in Timișoara, Romania, where my grandfather, grandmother and aunt are buried, where my parents will one day be buried, but not me (I want to burn), my mother spends a lot of time caring for the graves. Honoring the dead. Bringing crowns of flowers to the graves. Even now, when she can no longer go there herself, she sends her cousin Lia to place the crowns on the graves of her father, mother, and sister on The Day of the Dead.

In my early childhood, my mother and I would go to this very cemetery together, it was our weekend ritual. We would light up candles. Fighting the wind to get them to burn. Bringing fresh flowers, plucking out the weeds. Praying.

Nowadays, she complains a lot, that I no longer care, that I am not religious anymore. "I care, but in a different way," I tell her.

She would do the same at home, caring for the flowers in our backyard. Planting flowers each spring. Plucking out the weeds.

A neighbor once asked her why would she keep doing this, the weeds will continue to grow anyway.

"Why do we shower then? The dirt will keep covering our bodies day by day anyway," she answered.

A wild rose is growing on my grandfather's grave, its roots and stem so strong, they break through stone.

Saying Goodbye

"Outside it is raining.
The earth calls its clouds
And they come, they come slowly
Because the earth belongs to no one."

– Iuliu Ioanovici

I wish I could've met my grandfather in person. We'd have many stories to tell each other, a lot of truth to challenge and share, things to talk about. I'll never hear the sound of his voice, see him smile, or know what it means to be held by him. But I'm carrying him inside me, in my mother's memories, and in my genes. There are words that bind us, and "the will, the character, and the temperament: the 3 factors that our happiness or unhappiness in life depends on."

Unlike the main characters of other books about oppression, my grandfather wasn't a true dissident. He wasn't a hero. Someone who stood up for or against an idea. He died for nothing. He wasn't a revolutionary protester. He didn't spread pamphlets. All he did was live his life. In the secret police records about him, many pages are blackened out. I guess we are still not supposed to know certain things.

His life and death were supposed to be erased by the social discourse of his time. He was supposed to be exterminated. Over nothing.

Somewhere among poems, diaries, family stories, and security records, lies the truth. The truth of my grandfather's brilliant mind and thirst for knowledge. The truth in our blood. The truth of his broken spleen. The truth of his life, love, and death. The truth I have tried to bring out.

While I am writing these lines, my mother is in bed; she fell and injured her back. She cannot walk, or even sit at the edge of the bed without help, and her memories are hazy, fading away, overlapping. Sometimes, she hallucinates. My grandmother was like this too, the weeks and months before she died. I am glad my mother and I got to talk about my grandfather and all the things that had been done to our family before this happened.

Last year, between Christmas and New Year, I interviewed her. She showed me all the materials she's been keeping hidden about him, inside the drawers next to her bed. She made sure I put all of them back after I hastingly read all of them, night after night, at the turn of the year. Back then, I didn't tell her about my intention to write a book about us, about him, about her. I still haven't told her. I couldn't bring myself to do it.

All her old attempts to write his and her story resulted in maniacal episodes, followed by debilitating, lengthy depressions. A total withdrawal from written or spoken words. While I was growing up, and even more so, after I became a writer, she would often tell me: "Be careful with what you write about; how honest you are; who you open up to; remember what happened to your grandfather. Remember!"

I feel like my grandfather's story and the way it shaped our family's (his)story and identity has cost my mother her life. I believe this story has been trying to come out for decades. Decades of silence and disease, eating away at people's bodies and souls.

It's easier for me to write a book about my mother, in a language she doesn't understand, than to tell her that I love her. Than to tell her I forgive her, for not being there, truly present, while I was growing up.

That I understand, all the things that her doctors never have, because she has always been too afraid to tell them what had been done to her, to them, to us; too afraid to talk to her therapist, who deemed her the most reluctant patient she has ever met and gave up on her early on.

The way I best care is through words. The words that so many before me could not say.

Our voices, my grandfather's, my mother's, and mine, they are alike. They are more alike than I thought they'd be when I started writing this book. They are alike when we suffer. But also, when we feel joy. And last but not least, they are alike when we write.

I will never know my grandfather in person. And yet, "the sun is so beautiful on some days, it spills its happiness with such intensity that you'd think you're dreaming and the reality of such a landscape isn't possible." On such days, what we share is almost enough.

Voice V – The Old and the New World

(Country; Fire)

Doi Ani Prea Devreme

I WATCH A movie called *15 noiembrie 1987 Brașov - Doi ani prea devreme (Two years too early)*, directed by Liviu Tofan. There is a street called November 15th in Brașov. In 2018-2019, people are interviewed on the street. Many do not know why the street is called like this, although they live there. But there are a few who do.

"Yes, I know why it is called like that, I was there, in the Tools section (*Unelte și Scule, Forjă*). It was hard to eat, to find food."

"They called the street like this so that people would not forget. The bread was sold out, those who would wake up at 8 am were lazy, they couldn't find bread anymore, it was sold out."

"I stopped at the bar *Select* to drink coffee like in those times, *nechezol*, it wasn't really coffee, you know, and to smoke a cigarette. On the boulevard I saw a column of people, like for *Defilare*, spread across the whole Lablaka street. And I couldn't even find bread to buy!"

"On the 11th of November, we had no food, no heating, and they gave us a shitty salary. We just couldn't take it anymore."

RO "*Ceaușescu a căzut de la etajul 2, l-au pus în picioare si i-au dat foc.*"

EN "Ceaușescu's photo fell from the second floor, they made him stand and set him on fire."

On November 15th 1987, thousands of workers from the truck factory *Steagul Roșu* (EN *The Red Flag*) in Brașov, an industrial platform the size of a city (having then 50,000 employees and spreading over tens of hectars) went out on the street, demanding not only food and heating, but also the fall of dictatorship. This freedom only lasted for a few hours, as the Secret Police quickly put a stop to the protest. By evening, hundreds of people had been arrested, sent into militia basements, beaten up, tortured, humiliated, and/or deported.

Protestul Diasporei

In August 2018, Romanians from abroad (I am not among them) return to Bucharest, Romania to protest against governmental corruption. Other protesters join them. They bring their children to the protests and when the police goes against the peaceful protesters with tear gas (which is especially harmful for children), they get blamed for being irresponsible parents. In the German press, the Romanians from Germany who travel to Romania to take part in the protest are described as *Gastarbeiter* (guest workers), the same terminology used for the Turks that helped rebuild Germany after WWII (Turks who were later accused of bringing their whole families to Germany and "not integrating"). Even in respectable newspapers such as *Der Spiegel (The Mirror)*, Romanian *Gastarbeiter* are described as seasonal workers and truck drivers. This is the terminology usually associated with Romania in the German press: beggars, *Gastarbeiter*, and thieves. Educated Romanians do not make the news because there is nothing sensational about that.

On the 10th of August 2018, peaceful Romanian protesters are silenced by being beaten and attacked with tear gas. Tear gas is also commonly used against migrant children in other parts of the world, to this day, for instance at the Mexico-US border.

"Gased in Our Own Country" are the new headlines in newspapers in Romania.

The police remain innocent.

"We did nothing wrong. All we did was follow orders."

The Harvest – *Spargelzeit*

In the spring of 2020, it is white asparagus season and there is a lot of white asparagus to harvest, like every year. In the middle of the pandemic, while in Romania itself people cannot go out farther than 2 kilometers from their homes, Romanian workers from a major Covid-19 epidemic center in Romania are brought to Germany to work the fields that Germans do not wish to work themselves. So-called *seasonal* Romanian *workers* are brought to Germany by plane to harvest the white asparagus that Germans love to eat so much. It seems that Germans are fit enough to go bouldering and climb mountains each weekend, but not to harvest their most beloved non-meat-based food, so the Romanian and German governments, in the spirit of EU solidarity, reach an agreement. The Romanian government, in the spirit of solidarity, sells the health and well-being of their cheap-labor, poor people to the German government. It does not matter that we are all part of the EU, that we are all white. It does not matter, because the EU is an economic, not a humanitarian alliance. And it is, as always, racist. It is about trade and people willing to work hard and risk their health for low income, if they have the misfortune of having been born in a poor country. It makes no difference if the job is to harvest white asparagus or plough cotton fields. Those who join one plantation (I mean asparagus farm) cannot leave it, they depend on their master, even if their master treats them poorly. They are forced to sleep together in one room, like back in those times, when Romanian or Romanian-German refugees made their way to Germany in illegality. They can only leave if they get sick. Then they do not get treated in Germany, instead they get sent "back home".

Nicolae Ceaușescu

THE DICTATOR WHOM I watched dying as a child (well, almost, as they did not show the exact milliseconds of his actual killing on TV) is not the same that my grandfather suffered and died under. That was Gheorghe Gheorghiu Dej, the first communist leader of Romania, who ruled the country from 1947 to 1965, in his position of General Secretary of the Romanian Communist Party (ultimately "Romanian Workers' Party" PMR).

During my time in Canada as *Worker – Biology*, I start writing a book about a small, old Romanian man, one who immigrates and then loses his daughter and grandchildren in a car crash. In a white land with overwhelmingly beautiful nature, where lakes, mountains, and rivers are larger and more spectacular than everything he has ever seen and they threaten to swallow him whole. This man is now on his own. He doesn't speak the same language as everyone else around him, but he is free. Free to do what he wants. He looks a lot like Nicolae Ceaușescu, a small, old version of him.

I meet a man like that on a long-distance Grayhound bus traveling from Jasper to Edmonton and wonder for a split second if it is him, if the shooting of my childhood is just a scam, and this is the real Nicolae Ceaușescu, sitting right in front of me, anonymously, riding the same bus. Then I do the math and it seems impossible – Ceaușescu was already in his 70s when he was killed in 1989.

You can tell from the way he looks that he is not from here, that he does not belong. He looks at me and I shiver. Then he looks away, but I look again, and we keep doing this for a while. Neither of us says a single word. We look like the only immigrants on this bus, lost in the wilderness of these vast Canadian mountain lands.

This man could've been my grandfather, had he lived. He could be one of my parents. Or the old Romanian man I helped fill out immigration forms at the Calgary airport when I first landed in Canada, who traveled all the way from his little village in Romania, via Frankfurt, to live with his daughter. And then, at the Calgary airport, he could not find her upon landing, so I went with him to the Information Center and placed an announcement for his daughter to come pick him up from there, which she did.

It could also be or have been me.

On some days, I feel like I have abandoned my parents to cut my own way through life. But don't we all do this eventually?

Not in Romania, there we don't. We stay and care for them and always put family first. Before our own needs. Without boundaries. Because for decades and decades, under communist rule, that is what it took to survive.

As my parents age, as I get older, there is more and more guilt to carry. And I cannot go on with this book in which everyone is free yet everyone dies.

This old man in the novel I never finish writing is the embodiment of depression in my family. He lives on a real street in Calgary, named Unwin Road. No matter what he does, he cannot win. He is starting to forget the names of things in his mother tongue while his English remains sketchy and imprecise and he needs to start placing stickers around his small flat, like a map of lost identity. This is a man who loses everything – language, family, purpose, and ultimately – his identity.

As I write this, I do not know my mother will be facing her own memory loss too soon.

When my father goes through his second hyponatremia, I watch *Still Alice*. I cope with my own pain by witnessing someone else's fictional pain, while I avoid dealing directly with my own. Because this is what I learned to do in my childhood – in times of stress, stay focused on problem-solving and shove down my feelings. In a family where others cannot take care of themselves, there is always one person who needs to be everyone's caretaker and *stay strong*.

This man is also the old man working at Tim Horton's as an usher. He opens doors for everyone, but nobody is there to open the door for him when he goes home. He forgets to smile and ultimately gets fired because he just opens doors and never asks "How are you today?" as he should. He cannot go through life as if all were just fine.

In other versions of the book, he is younger, an artist, one who seduces women and does not know how to let them get close. When one of them does, either their child dies, or she becomes a writer and they gradually drift away. Once she finds and owns her voice, his becomes smaller and loses its power. In others, she is only a mother and nothing more.

When my mother starts writing her father's story – my father tells her, the woman who supported his artistic career, to stop, because she lacks literary talent. I never discuss the matter of talent with him, but I generally keep away from painting. I do not wish to be compared with him.

I never finish this novel. I write a story about an artist instead. The woman in the story is blind, but she affirms her power inside his world – by painting her own self-portrait with her entire body, using her arms and legs, on the canvas on the floor. And then she lets him touch her, but not like he used to. She goes from being an object in his world to being a subject. She lets herself be seen although she herself cannot see anymore and seeing is his power. Touching becomes hers. And, in the world of the story, she is the actual artist, not him – because she reinvents herself despite her aging, loss, and disabilities.

In the beginning of the novel I never finish, there is a man; he is old and traveling alone through Canada. A small, anonymous Ceaușescu, whom people neither know nor worship. A small, almost invisible man, one who will not mark history in a dominant way. With his shephard hat or baseball cap that doesn't fit, it doesn't matter. An ordinary man.

Trapped in the past. Alone. Or: His family died. He is alone. He has Alhzeimer's. He forgot how to smile. But this is not the real story.

The Nostalgics

THERE ARE ALSO other people in Romania. Those who went to weep at Ceaușescu's grave, decades later. Those who followed Gheorghe Gheorghiu Dej, when it all started. Twenty-seven years after Ceaușescu's death, some people still gather at his grave, recite poems, drink Coca-Cola, fight each other, and nostalgically talk about how good things used to be "before" (in Romania we still often talk about life before and after the fall of Communism, the way Christians record time by talking about the time before and after Christ). How people used to have secure jobs for life, but we were stupid and we killed Ceaușescu only to become seasonal workers elsewhere (picking up strawberries in Spain or building houses for others in Germany). Some say that Donald Trump wanted to buy *Casa Poporului* (*The House of the People*) in Bucharest, which I can understand, because it is, after all, the kind of building that Trump would call "a great house!" An old woman is holding a newspaper with the headline "Ceaușescu, Reimbodied in a Little Boy in Galați." Hope dies last. At the end, everyone eats *colivă*.

Then, there are those born after 1989 who never experienced the transition from communism to "democracy" (the democracy of "tear gas for your children"). Some of them do not know why there is a street in my home town Timișoara, the martyr town (where everything started back in 1989), called *Bulevardul 16 Decembrie 1989*. There are also those whose parents do not talk to them about the life before.

Some of those born after 1989 dream of becoming communists. In 2013, it was found that 38% of the teenagers born after 1989 thought that things had been better in communism than during the so-called *transition period* they were in. (I do not remember when we stopped talking about the *transition period* in Romania.)

It seems that those growing up in poor families or in the countryside were more predisposed to such nostalgia for a time they have never themselves experienced than those from middle class families or growing up in the city. In addition, those with parents with a low to medium level of education were also more inclined to assessing communism as better than the present day. Last but not least, those who had traveled outside Romania were less likely to come up with such an assessment. Five kids in this article are members of the current Romanian Communist Party.

In December 2019, I read an article in the German newspaper *Der Spiegel* about Ion Iliescu (who once headed the *Front of the National Salvation*) being under investigation for crimes against humanity in December 1989, when people continued being shot for no good reason. Even after Ceaușescu's arrest. It is a long article.

For a very long time afterwards, I hear nothing about the topic. But after the fiasco with the Belarus elections in the summer of 2020, I ask my father about it during one of our video calls. He shrugs his shoulders and says: "Nothing happened, they couldn't gather enough evidence."

Voice VI – Mia's End

(Earth; Doors)

The Tracks

Life and death, two parallel lines.
In between you –
This body you cannot escape.

Illness

It is November 2019. Now, my father takes care of my mother. Every day, she is asking for me: "When can we go see Diana?" or "When is Diana coming home?".

She doesn't remember that I don't live there anymore. I go visit. I take care of her as if she were my child, my precious child, and I tell her that I love her, over and over again. My mother's brain, despite its atrophic condition, is much stronger than she thinks, though. She is more strong-willed than she realizes. Her brain, her will to live, they are still fighting to keep her alive. In her hallucinations, she is tender, optimistic, witty, and full of love. She doesn't see her father, but she often sees my grandmother and my aunt. Sometimes, she thinks I am my aunt, her beloved elder sister.

"My mother's image comes to me so often these days," she tells me. "I see so many scenes, so many moments from your childhood. I see her cooking in the kitchen for you. Baking apple and pumpkin pie, making pancakes."

"Your presence is better than all the doctors," my mother tells me. "It is OK if you don't want to have children, but please find a partner, don't live alone." And she goes on: "I want to bring you only joy from now on, no more trouble. No more pain. Don't be sad because of me," she tells me every day. "Don't worry

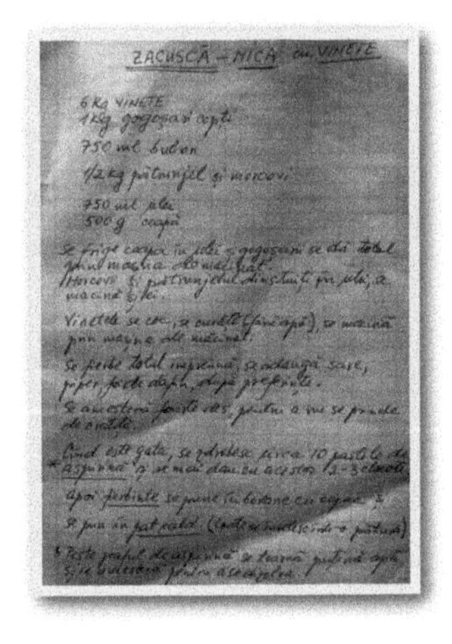
ZACUSCĂ – NICA cu VINETE

6 Kg VINETE
1 Kg gogoșari copți
750 ml bulion
1/2 kg pătrunjel și morcovi
750 ml ulei
500 g ceapă

about me, focus on getting better," I say. And then I ask her: "How many mothers do I have?" She looks at me and smiles. And I say: "Only one." There is no resentment left, no more pondering over all the feelings, things, people, and moments that had been lost, only love.

Disconnection

Layers of scar tissue unfold under the microscope.
It is here that I seek beauty,
In the darkness.
The images need magnifying
To bring out the truth.
We carry many truths within our bodies.
Animals naturally shake to release trauma.
Sometimes, we forget.
Our bodies remember
And our brains try to hold on.
Disconnections flutter.
Lesions in our white matter
Affect our perception of time.
The past becomes tomorrow.
A dead mother becomes a presence.

Mia's Death

MY MOTHER DIES during the pandemic. She dies on the 21st of August 2020, and I turn 38 on the 30th of August. At her funeral, in the same cemetery where her father, mother, and sister are buried, and Aunt Feli, too, we all wear masks. Some of my mother's friends and cousins come to drop off flower crowns, as imposed by tradition, before the actual funeral, but do not stay for the ceremony. There is a lot of freshly dug soil, removed from the graves of my mother's uncle and aunt *Drăghici*. Their bones are placed in a sack by the undertaker, to make room for my mother's coffin at the bottom, and later, for my father's, at the top, in who knows how many years, very likely not that many. There are parts of the ritual I do not know or do not remember; the last funeral I attended was in 2002 and my aunt's, but there are also many parts that I know. I know them because they haven't changed over time and my mother's retelling of her father's death was so vivid in her writing that it is forever ingrained in the visual part of my brain.

They are covering the coffin, they are digging nails into the coffin, they are lifting the coffin, they are lowering the coffin into the freshly dug soil, the priest is pouring red wine over the coffin. I do not see the undertakers cover the coffin with the soil because I need to be somewhere else in the graveyard to give away *colaci* (they look like Challah) and *colivă*. With a friend, I go to my grandfather's grave to light up a candle. The candle is tall and once lit it burns the marble ceiling, but we let it. It burns and burns. The candles the funerary convoy hold in their hands at my mother's funeral do not burn that long, half of them die out. It is a hot and windy day. With the same friend, I go back to my mother's grave afterwards, where all the flower crowns are set at the top. The tombstone is not to be placed yet, the chief undertaker says that the earth needs to settle over the grave first, it is too moist, it needs to press on the grave.

When I choose the coffin at the funeral parlor, I choose it by color. A reddish brown that was among my mother's favorite colors. I choose the one called Rosé. It has a rose on the lid. I think about my grandfather's grave rose, the one that broke through stone.

My mother is not buried with the rest of her direct family but on the other side of the chapel, where my father's name is also already engraved in stone, with his birth year. Only his death year is still missing. Hers is freshly engraved: 2020.

I can no longer see the blood shot eyes of her dead body, I will never see them again. At home, after the funeral, I finally sleep, a sleep without dreams. The day before I sort out old photos, photos from before her depression, and also from after. From before her first fall in more recent years, and also from after.

The priest reads the entire eulogy that my father and I wrote. I tell my father about the book that I am writing. The eulogy he drafts and I edit talks about my grandfather's death as a life-long scar on my mother, and about the humiliations that her family endured both before and after his return from prison. It is the first time that the details of her family's trauma are read publicly in Romania, by a priest no less. My father and I joke before the funeral: based on the details he will choose to leave out, we'll know his political orientation. But the priest is young and he reads all of it. I cry when he does.

There are no beggars at my mother's funeral during the pandemic. A few days later, I watch a documentary about Nina Simone, who also had bipolar disorder/manic depression. In one interview, she says: "They do not know that I died and what they are seeing is my ghost." I tell my friend Alina that this is how I feel about my mother

– that I lost her when I was 12, not now, and only her ghost has been around for all these years, but now her ghost has finally found its way out.

After my mother's death, I feel her absence, but her absence is light. Her lying in bed for so many years during my childhood and also during her last 2 years of life, that was heavy. I feel sad but I am grieving less than before. It was her presence with all the pain trapped inside her body that was heavy. When she dies, I feel calm for the first time in years. Things begin to settle. Like the earth on her grave.

A few days later, I realize that I will never again hear her voice and that I don't have any recording of it. I find this thought upsetting. Why didn't I think of it before? I remember people calling us at home, back when I was still in high-school or a university student, and mistaking my voice for my mother's. Except that one time a school friend told me: "I always know it is you and not her because she is more polite than you when she picks up."

My father copes with grief by being insulting and controlling. After a few days, he finally changes the linen on what used to be my mother's bed. He was alone with her when she died. I was still boarding at the Munich airport when she died.

Now, he cannot stand the silence. He wants me to stay with him evenings before he falls asleep. Like a child. Neither of us sits on her bed. It still smells. "A mixture of disinfectant and urine," I say. "Corpse smell," he says. "I cannot recover," he tells me. "I want to recover to paint. But I cannot."

My father tells me stories about my mother each time we speak, and especially at night. From her last months, but also from their first years together. One evening, I think he almost stops doing it, but then he starts again. He tries to make jokes at times, jokes that involve her and are half-sinister, but it doesn't always work.

He cries the first night and says I yell at him without a reason. It is not me doing the yelling. It's his own loss and pain.

One night, my father dreams that he gets off the tram, at the tram stop close to our home, but once he takes a few steps away from the stop, walking towards our old home, he realizes my mother isn't there. He had lost her. He goes back to the tram stop but she is gone, the tram is gone. In his dream, he goes to his studio to find her but can't. He had lost her.

That morning, after the dream, it rains heavily and we need to disconnect the power supplies. Sometimes the internet or TV get damaged during a storm here. I ask him: "Do you remember back in my childhood, when the water would pile up on the street like a river during a summer storm, because the water canalization system wasn't working? Do you remember how the 3 of us – you, me, and *mama* – would put old cloth pieces in the windows, to prevent water from pouring into our house, but it would still pour in through the walls?" And he says: "Yes, we had old wooden windows back then."

He also doesn't know what we should do with the 10 hectares of forest that the Romanian state returned to our family (after the fall of communism) now that my mother died. We do not use the wood to sell it. I do not want to sell it or give it away.

On my birthday, he tells my cousin that he wants to give it back to the state. My cousin calls me to tell me Happy Birthday but ends up begging me not to let the state retrieve the land. "The state that peed on our family," is the wording he uses.

This is where I'm from.

I assure him that I won't. He tells me about the photos he found of my grandfather in Brestovăț, where the forest we own is also located. The same way he sent me Google maps snapshots of our ancestors' graves (so that I know where my mother should be buried), he says he will send me snapshots of our land. The forest where we share land.

An aunt who comes to the funeral, one of my mother's cousins, Lia, the 81-year old still living daughter of Aunt Feli (both Lia and aunt Feli are actually named Ofelia, the drowning princess, with the shorter forms Lia and Feli) comes to visit my dad and me 1 day after my 38th birthday. Her sister committed suicide a few years ago. Her daughter has terminal cancer (but, somehow, partially recovers one year later). Her son lives in Munich, like me. It is where I met him for the first time back in 2016. He and I have been meeting at least a couple of times per year since then. It is he and his sister who inform me of my mother's microcerebral attacks, after their mother visits my parents in 2018 and my dad is overwhelmed by the situation, but clearly in denial. It is through them that we buy my mother almost 2 last years of so-called living.

My aunt asks me, looking at the portraits of my grandfather, grandmother, and mother, the ones above my father's bed, facing the armchair that she is sitting in:

"How old was Mia in that picture?"

"Maybe 17, 18, she must have just finished high-school here or perhaps she was already a student," I say.

"Ah, your grandfather Iuliu, what a personality! How much life advice he gave Mia, how much they loved each other, how close they were! What a pity you never met him! You and Iulie would have been on the same wavelength, on so many things."

It is an unexpected gift, hearing this about him from someone from our extended family. She is one of the few family members still alive and old enough to have met him, to remember him, and to share stories about him.

Then she goes on: "When he was in hospital, at Bega – it wasn't a maternity ward back then – I baked sour cherry pie for him. I brought it to him and begged him to eat it. But he just said: *I am sorry, but I can't. I have no appetite.*"

My grandfather was terminally ill in the same hospital where I was born, 2 decades later.

Then she goes on: "My mother Feli went to see him and the doctor told her: *Never in my entire career have I seen a man with all of his organs so damaged inside*. And he never talked about what happened to him in detention, out of fear. He never talked about it." She repeats it, the missing puzzle piece: "He never talked about it." We will never fully know.

So, when people ask me: "Where do you come from?"

I want to tell them: "I come from this land, who did this to my grandfather, my family. Who made my mother take her high-school leaving exam in the subject Socialism, while her father was rotting in his grave as a result of that very same dogmatic system. Who made her teach me patriotic songs and poems when I was in Kindergarten and primary school and I was just learning to read and write. Who, in the 80s, made my father paint a portrait of Elena Ceaușescu, the dictator's wife, with threats that if he does not do it, if he just goes on painting psychedelic stuff, there will be consequences for him and his family." But, oftentimes, I still don't. I say "Romania" with a bitter smile on my face and do not tell them more than that. Because, most of the times, this is all they are willing to hear.

I end up writing and rewriting the answer, and I do it for myself in the end more than I do it for anyone else. I need this answer much more than they do, the real answer. I stubbornly keep hoping that if I do my homework well, one day all this framing and reframing will somehow make sense or lead to a different outcome, one that will be my true Northern Star from now on. Or at least allow me to find and keep my center.

When I first started writing this book, I thought it would mostly be about my mother's trauma. I thought I would untangle all the things I didn't know about my grandfather. I had no idea it had caused such a ripple effect across our entire extended family. I had no idea it was just a huge, unconscious part of my own fractured identity. Of my lifelong anxiety, insecurity, and desire to prove myself, even if it meant doing things I didn't enjoy. Like getting straight A's in all subjects in school, even those I hated or that somehow didn't really matter. Of my desire to write, without knowing what to write about. When I was 27, I wanted to finish writing a book before hitting 30. I wrote a PhD thesis in biophysical chemistry instead. When I was 28, back in early 2010, my life fell apart in Canada and I went back to the writing I had left off when I first moved to Germany, back in 2004. In my very first creative writing class in Calgary, I was writing fictionalized personal narratives, projecting myself into my female characters. My teachers would say: too much disease, too much loss, too many problems for a single short story. Zoom in on one. I was confused: wasn't life always full of problems rather than just one? My teachers also mentioned that memoir was becoming a popular genre. The idea of ever writing and publishing memoir seemed so foreign. Why would anyone other than a narcissist do that?

I thought I would be writing about my mother and grandfather, to bring their words and experiences to life. I didn't know this book would end up also being about me claiming my space, on the page and in the world.

The same day that my aunt Lia visits my father and me, I discover my diary from 1993. One year before my mother was fired, diagnosed, and everything changed. I wrote there about us going to the cinema together. About the days when she would still visit her aging mother to care for her. To make sure my grandmother wouldn't fall. My grandmother's ending and my mother's were similar: with dementia, in bed, living in the past, seeing things that were not there. Except that my grandmother passed away much faster than my mother.

My mother loved without boundaries or conditions. In the process, she annihilated herself and her own needs to better serve the needs of our family. Until she broke. She loved in a way I both can and can't. I won't. I'd love a child like this perhaps, but never again a man.

Or, would I still? Is that what women seek, more through

nurture than through nature, a man and children they can surrender themselves to? This isn't what I'd logically seek as a life of meaning. But that doesn't mean I fully stop craving it. After all this searching, all this reframing, a part of me still wants to be chosen to surrender.

Body (II)

It reeks of death over and near and inside the bed
Where her body was left for several hours until
The morgue people came and
Took what was left of the body away.
The body was kept in the freezer and layers of makeup
Were applied onto what was once her face.
The body was dressed into
So-called earth colors.
The body that she
Could no longer possess.
The body was left uncovered for
The ceremony no one believed in.
Makeup was wrongly placed.
Her eyes were red between her eyelids, bloodshot.
The body was placed on wheels,
Nails were dug into the coffin
That had a rose on the lid that would at first not close.
The body was locked inside the coffin
And lowered to the bottom of the grave.
Wine was thrown over the coffin
Hosting what used to be a body.
Earth was left to pour,
Flowers were left
To rot
On top.

Things That Are Heavy and Light

My mother used to tell me that if I put a seashell next to my ear I can hear the sea, the sound of the waves. This year is the first in many when I do not get to see the sea or the ocean. The last ocean I saw was on the Isle of Skye. The last sea, in Inverness. The North Sea. I remember walking alone in the rain through muddy grounds, facing the wind and the rain, and feeling like this was it, freedom, the only thing I really needed.

All my life, my body has been trying to take up more space than it was supposed to. To tell a story bigger than that of one self only. To take up the space that my ancestors could not take. To be broad and tall and nothing like the delicate tiny woman cliché.

My mother was once delicate. I am not. As a child I was sicklish and thin, but I was always tall. I was shy and lacked self-confidence and didn't know why I was like that, but later it all made sense, once I untangled and almost understood my mother's story.

8 September 2020

Today would've been my mother's 73rd birthday and Name Day. I start the day by ligthning a candle in the dark, watching the sunrise, and then, after breakfast, I fight with my dad. I still need to fight him for my space, my needs, my boundaries. He copes with grief by being controlling, by sticking to and imposing his routine. I cope with grief in silence, by myself. Watching the clouds, writing about them. Staying alive, in the moment, whatever that moment brings.

A woman I know in Munich who has no children but comes from my home town, whose family grave is close to that of my mother, is born on the same day and year as my mother. I find this out via FB on what would've been my mother's 73rd birthday. She tells me – when hearing the news of my mother's death – that all her family is there, behind the chapel, and that she has nobody to carry her family's name forward. No children after her death.

At times I think of her as something like an adoptive mother. She was there last year when I read my text out loud at Gasteig about the fall of communism from a child perspective. We took photos together before the reading. Many people were there, people who knew me in my childhood, or who knew my parents when they were all young, "back home." Many generations who have left Romania and moved to Germany in the 70s, 80s, or 90s. And some born after 1989. With their children and grandchildren.

The Chapel

It is late September 2020 and one month since my mother died when I revisit the cemetery and her grave. The crowns of flowers on her grave are all dried out and the rock-solid lid has not been placed over her grave yet, because the earth still needs to settle. There are plants growing in what is supposed to be the stone vase of her grave, so I use a half-cut plastic bottle instead. I insert the flowers I bought at the grocery store (the only place I found selling flowers at this time of day), a mixture of roses, something yellow, and something white. Flowers I cannot name, except for the rose. The rose looks strong. I light up candles. Like I used to do with her in my childhood.

How much pain can one body hold before it breaks the brain? How much pain can a physical space hold? The place in front of the graveyard chapel is just a place, empty of meaning. Filled with the pain of so many. But when they leave, it's just empty, just a place like any other. Only the traces of burnt candle light on the ground speak of something that was lost.

At my mother's funeral, the place in front of the chapel is full of people wearing masks and I am not sure if having them around is

really helping me. I feel like this is a show that needs to be put on for the world to adhere to traditions, but not how I would prefer to grieve. I am not religious and going through a ceremony I don't believe in is the last thing I want to do to say goodbye to her in such a public and prescripted way. Even though I haven't attended a funeral since 2002, even though I do not believe in a Christian God or any other God, I hold the ritual because I know this is what she would've wanted. My mother who spent years paying for her burial place at the cemetery, saving money for the funeral. Money that she has stored safely somewhere in her and my father's flat, so safely that we can't find it anymore. The singing at my mother's funeral is not as bad as I thought it would be. I can see how incantations can work in a healing way, even if they are old Orthodox ones. Many people are uncomfortable feeling or talking about grief, but with singing, all they must do is listen.

I go through the ritual but I do not kiss her body before they dig the nails into the coffin and take it to her grave. Our souls part here. The soil is fresh and wet. There is so much soil, too much. The priest pours red wine over the coffin. When I leave the cemetery that evening in late September, one month after her funeral, the *pietrar* is marking new names and years on graveyard stones, close to the cemetery gate. The sound he makes is the only sound I hear in the graveyard that day. I talk to my mother's undertaker before her funeral and also at the funeral. I give him and his team "of boys" *țuică de casă*. They expect this kind of bribe. Home-made alcoholic *țuică* and money. In addition to the official funeral fee. Without it they wouldn't dig the grave. Wouldn't put the bones of my mother's aunt and uncle in a sack, wouldn't place her coffin at the bottom, to make room at the top for my father, for when his death will come. I talk to her undertaker again, not in the cemetery, but on the street. He passes by and asks me, without showing any signs of recognizing me:

"Are you making a film of old things on your way?"

"No, I tell him, I am taking photos. Of old doors, houses, and windows." He looks at me and looks at the doors from the turn of the century:

"They no longer make them like this," he tells me. "Maybe in *Maramureș*, but not here."

"A pity," I say, "isn't it? They really no longer make them this way."

Then he is on his way. I take one last photo and leave.

Motherhood

When my mother dies, my desire to become a mother is stronger than ever. A desire that I never expected to feel so intensely, which took off at the start of the pandemic. I tell my doctor friend that I am probably running out of *ovule*, that this desire is purely biologic, organic. I feel it from deep within myself, my body, I feel it when I am in nature, in the heart of the forest, and everything around me seems to be squirming with life, with the sun pouring between the trees and the surface of the ground half-lit. There in the dim light I feel alive.

I picture it, my daughter and me, in the mountains, just the 2 of us. Laughing at each other.

I will perhaps one day adopt a girl from a Romanian orphanage, a girl that nobody wanted. A little girl, not a baby. And one day, when she will be 12, I will be there for her and everything will be alright.

It is time for a new family narrative.

Patruzeci de Zile – Forty Days

It is almost 40 days since my mother's death as I am wrapping up this chapter of my book, back in Munich, while my father plans the so-called *pomană* (giving food to poor people at church) back in Romania. It is said – in Orthodox tradition – that the soul of the deceased person lingers among the loved ones for 40 days. It is also after 40 days that Jesus ascended to Heavens and 40 days is the official duration of pre-Christmas and pre-Easter fasts for the religious.

It is a sunny day in Munich, one of the few lately, and fall has fully settled in. I go to the old Winthirkirche church and cemetery in my neighborhood; both have been there since the Middle Ages and don't quite belong in the contemporary landscape of the neighborhood. I light up candles for the dead, and I light up some for the living too – my mother, my aunt, my uncle, my grandfather, my grandmother, my cousin, my father, and me.

I walk into the cemetery where graves are not rock-solid like in Romania, but rather made of earth, sometimes with flowers of all colors growing on top. I walk to the very end of the small cemetery. It is so much smaller than most of the cemeteries here.

On the same day, my hometown in Romania gets a new mayor, Dominic Fritz, born and raised in Germany, in a large family, in the Black Forest, near the springs of the Danube.

I remember the postcards of Timișoara my mother would still send me in 2016, when her hands were shaking heavily but she could

still hold a pen and write, before she started falling for no apparent reason.

A pregnant black cat crosses my path. She heads straight to the sculpture with several figures merging into one another, like a family gathering. She keeps walking into the bushes and stays there, with the sun over her fur. She looks at me and smiles as cats do – with her eyes.

I leave through the back gate, into a side street, the sun shining on my face. I allow it to warm me up on my way.

Voice VII – New Beginnings, Possible Endings

(Air)

Longing

I

I am tired of always writing about the *I* that cannot be framed.
There are ways to surround this magic we call reality
But they escape me over and over and over again.
I have to start again from scratch,
My scraped knees tremble.
How many times must I climb the same mountain
Only to find a path, any path
Back into my real self
Beyond this thing called life, called longing?
Why must I always come back to *I*?
Like this I know I am still here,
I am still wanting, fighting for my life
Despite everything, despite my ancestors.
Despite. I am still walking, standing.
I am still a raw voice.

She

She is tired of always writing about the *she* that cannot be framed.
There are ways around this magic they call reality
But they escape her over and over and over again.
She has to start from scratch,
Her scraped knees tremble.
How many times must she climb the same mountain
Only to find a path, her path
Back into her real self
Beyond this thing called life, called longing?
Why must she always come back to herself?
Like this she knows she is still there,
She is still wanting, fighting for her own life
Despite everything, despite her ancestors.
Despite. She is still walking, standing,
She is still her own raw voice.

I Live in Words

I live in words,
between the pages of books
too old to be remembered.
When the lake ran dry,
We stopped spending our holidays there.
The lake became a myth.
Words became memories.
My body has traveled.
Country after country,
Everyone asked me:
Where is home?
Beyond language, beyond borders.
In mountains, and trees,
And the depths of the ocean.
I live in woods,
In lingering in-between places
Older than language.

Carry You Home

Let the water carry you home
to the source, the ancient bird song
of the ground underneath the stones.

Let the bones of your ancestors
hug you with stories of their own;
listen, and let them take you home.

Let the old forest trees whisper
all the secrets only they still know;
listen to the story below.

Let your muscles, arms, and ankles
guide your voice and truth into words of your own;
keep walking up and towards.

Let the water carry you home
to the high air of the mountains;
be the bird wings reclaiming their song.

Wolf

A wolf visits my dreams
and tells me about the crossing
to the other world,
one of joy but also of constant hunger.

On the moon it doesn't matter
if I am or not the wolf–
we are not enemies
and we are not water.

The wolf in my dreams
is not in the forest
but in my room.
I am a little girl on a chair.

Later I write about the girl
who lives in the hollow of a tree
and is the healer of the forest,
the girl who runs with the wolves.

The girl becomes the High Priestess
and when all wolves die
hunted down by evil humans
she creates a new forest.

Lenggries, Bayern, Germany

RO
„Cele rele să se spele,
Cele bune să se-adune."
(Zicală românească)

EN
"May the bad things get washed away,
May the good things gather."
(Romanian saying)

IN THE DEPTH of winter, during the peak of the second wave of the pandemic, right before Christmas, in 2020, a time when other people gather with their human families, I move to the village of Lenggries. Nested between the Alps, surrounded by forests, rivers, and streams. A place full of tradition and longstanding family connections, where registration at the townhall involves presenting your *Stammbaum – arborele genealogic* – your bloodline, your family tree (if you are from here, that is, or from a nearby village). I live in a new house that is meant to look old, close to the old village church with its sun clock and cemetery, where locals in traditional Bavarian clothing (which, in contrast to what Oktoberfest fans may think, goes beyond *Lederhosen* and sexy *Dirndls*) engage in weekly rituals I know little about.

A few weeks before that, I write a text about a woman who chooses to live a life that others may not understand. In a place far away from humans, but deeply rooted in nature.

She would go live in that house in the wilderness, that house that looked nothing like a home at all. There were no traces of human life left in it and at night it was haunted by the winds, but not by evil spirits. She knew that place would be her home as soon as she saw it. It was as if she could remember seeing it before, in a movie perhaps, a movie about a woman that was and wasn't her or like her, that could've been her in a previous life. She could not help thinking of witches, but there would be no witchcraft here, only writing, and nature, for nature was the source of all her being, of all her writing, of all her written magic, if you will. Here, where other people rarely made their way, here at the top, she felt like she could finally be herself and fulfill her life's mission, to bring voice to so many things left unsaid for far too long. It wasn't the usual kind of fertility that her female voice and body would pour into the world, but it was her calling.

Unlike her, I do not live on the peak of a mountain, but in a valley. I do not need to hunt or pluck my own food. But I could be that woman, one day. I could also be another woman, one who *mothers* and *wives, actively* and *proactively*, like most women of our time still do, or are expected to.

Mother-nature. Here, I often find myself thinking of the Mother I had lost so many times throughout my life, times when I had to learn and relearn to both be her mother and to mother myself.

All countries have stories and myths about mythical water creatures: *Lostrița, Mica Sirenă și alți monștrii subacvatici*. There are many stories about people living on the borderlands, between earth and water. Old Dutch fairytales, Aquaman, but also many modern stories. In one of them, a woman from the surface moves to live underneath the sea with the man she loves.

I move to the Alps to live by myself, leaving the men I once loved in the city. I am not a true country girl, but this is where I find peace and home. Mountains, forests, trees, rivers, lakes, chimneys, fire, wood, smoke, scent, chirping birds, hawks, and endangered birds, laying their eggs on the islands of the river Isar, views of valleys – they surround me and are always there. I feel like being wrapped in a cocoon that is never too tight and leaves plenty of space for both discovery and longing.

Stories of water are the same everywhere. Like stories of loss. I choose to live in a village on the river Isar, in a valley, among mountain ranges. I choose a river, not a lake. A river that always flows and has islands untouched by humans. A river that originates in Austria and travels through Bavaria, through my chosen village, before making its way into the Danube, reentering Austria, flowing all the way to Hungary, Romania, and eventually into the big Black Sea, which I once thought would be black, but it turned out to be just deep blue. The accumulation lake Sylvensteinsee meets the Isar only 15 km away from Lenggries. Like many accumulation lakes, it occasionally runs dry, exposing the sacrifices once made for it to be born. Traces of the sunk village become visible then. But for most of the year all we see is its beauty. It looks natural, pristine. When it doesn't, we recall local myths and legends of loss.

Lenggries is a place that has character, like a fairytale. It is both cozy and alive with air. Houses are small and broad, made of wood, the same wood that is also the main source of trade and income here. All houses are spaced out and have spacious gardens. It is impossible to get the suffocating feeling created sometimes by too many tall buildings, side by side, which cities so often are made of. Size-wise Lenggries could qualify as a town, but it is kept a village on purpose, its aspect rustic, charming, traditional, but open. It is a place known for its tourism under non-pandemic conditions, but even then, it remains low-key.

The Isar can only be navigated by small boats here and there. One theory is that the name *Isar* comes from the hypothetical Indo-European root **es* or **is*, which generally meant "flowing water" and later turned into a word with a meaning narrowed to frozen water (hence English *ice*, German: *Eis*) in Proto-Germanic. An older theory is that it comes from Celtic words and the name *Isar* is a construction of the Celtic stems *ys* "fast, torrential" and *ura* "water, river" (*ura* means hatred in Romanian). According to another interpretation *ys* may mean "high" as well as "low", referring to the rapidly changing water level in the river Isar. In the ancient settlement area of the Celts, several related river names can be found: *Jizera* (Czech Republic), *Isère* (France), *Isel* (Austria), *IJseel* (Netherlands; known to Romans as *Isala*); *IJzer* (Belgium), *Eisack / Isarco* (Italy), *Isauro* (Italy), *Isonzo* (Italy), *Isar* (town in Spain), *Ésera* (Spain). The ancient name of the lower part of the river Danube, Ister, may have the same source. A friend tells me that Isar is also a word in her mother tongue, Farsi. It means selfless, altruistic, all the things I tried to escape and not be for so long.

We all spoke the same language once. One where nature was at the core of everything. Nature doesn't care where I'm from. Trees always impress me with their massive roots growing around rocks despite lacking proper grounding. They find a way. From underneath the earth, with open arms towards the sky.

Everything here coexists and is related. Water is lifegiving, like a form of birth. Rivers are in motion and can dry out in summer, but never forever. Rivers can change course, but water always chooses the shortest way. Water has over a hundred anomalies. We, humans, are 70% percent water, like our Earth.

Trees grow in families, rarely alone. Other plants grow on them. Birds nest at their top. Growth and transformation are unstoppable in the forest. They happen everywhere: underground, just above the surface, but also, in the air. The wind, the birds, the bees, and the butterflies. Spreading the seeds. For new life to emerge.

Here, I learn to sometimes be air and fire, not only earth and water. The pull of the earth is often still there. As seasons alternate repeatedly between winter and spring, this pull seems stronger than ever. To stay anchored, I keep obsessing over all the things growing underneath the snow. There are many flowers starting to sprout, only to find themselves buried again under new snowfalls.

It snows the weekend of the spring equinox, and it will still snow weekends after.

And yet, I am healthier and calmer than I have been in decades. And I can wait, for whatever will find its way out from underneath the snow.

Chronology (I)

Draft 1

Summer solstice. Familes gather around the fire, exhange pleasantries, eat.
I look at them from a distance. The hot flames cannot touch me.
Summer light passes through the window I left open
Before forgetting who I was.

Draft 2

Summer solstice. Families are gathering around the fire,
They are exchanging pleasantries, they are eating.
I keep looking at them from a distance.
The hot flames are not touching me.
Summer light is passing through the window
I had left open before, forgetting who I was.

Draft 3

Summer solstice. Families gathered around the fire,
Exchanged pleasantries, ate. I kept looking at them from a distance.
Their hot flames could not touch me.
Summer light passed through the window I had left open before,
Having forgotten who I once was.

Draft 4

Summer solstice. Families will be gathering around the fire, exchanging pleasantries, eating. I shall keep looking at them from a distance. Their hot flames will not touch me. Summer light will be passing through the window I will have left open before forgetting who I was.

Draft 5

Summer solstice. It will be as if families are gathering around the fire, exchanging pleasantries, eating. As if I'll keep looking at them from a distance. As if these hot flames won't be touching me. As if summer light were passing through the window I had left open, long before remembering who I once was.

Dreams

I scatter against dreams as doves gather among eagles.
Sand trembles across the ocean despite the running rollercoaster
We call longing. A noun collapses like a mistake.

The symptoms of love leaving the scenery.
A ladybug. A mermaid. Gathering at the bottom.
Chasing down memory through the family of things.

—~—

I find myself among dreams as trees let go of shadows.
Light merges with my hands turned green
Into mornings. A deer raises her head.

We do not know our endings.
A root. A wave. Ashes re-catching fire.
Spreading their tongues like invisible wings.

Body (III)

You becomes *I* when you surrender,
Love becomes possible.
The limbs of that little girl
Too tall, too shy, too skinny –
Never exactly what the world expected
Grew into this possibility
That you now call existence
As walking the earth becomes tomorrow,
As remembering life and family
Becomes you.

The hawk lands in hunger
And the forest remains standing.
Look at that cliff,
The trees growing around it,
Grabbing it with all their power,
Their roots in full expansion.
Look at yourself,
There is a mirror everywhere.
The entire world echoes,
I, I, I, here, alive.

Chronology (II)

FRACTURED BONES PLACE themselves back together. A spine chord, a rib cage, a mouth, wide open.

This is a place to which I want to always return. Sort it out, another life, space and time irrelevant.

My body is my home and it belongs to me alone. In it I carry memories that are my own, but also some of those before me. They are just memories, not trauma.

I am still all pieces, all pieces, all pieces, but they can be rearranged to build a whole. A whole from many holes.

Moments all blend into each other.

I am a mouth and I am also ears.

Here I am welcome.

Nobody needs to teach me how to breathe.

The secrets are no longer secrets because they are public.

I am not just history repeating itself.
It is OK to take up space.

We know how he died, what they did to him in prison.

Nobody ever told her to shut up, to make herself small.

Her body is never shrinking or falling, endlessly falling.

She stands up, washes her hair by herself, and eats.

We are all connected and part of the same big family.

Family. Family. Family.

It is better this way. There is no other way, anyway.

It is OK to move on, or to stay.

Space, time, everything, together.

I does not need to be *I*.

Neither of them ever grows old.

It is possible to leave but nobody wants to.

I can write about myself but don't have to, the story does not need to be unearthed, uncovered. Erasure and oppression never existed, they are concepts invented inside the caged world. There is no need to pursue an intellectual connection.

All there is is this – today, tomorrow, it does not matter.

There is nothing to hold on to or let go of.

It is just you and I climbing mountains together. You have never left this place we now both call home. Your eyes are big like the universe. We breathe in different languages, but it does not matter.

Between us a new breath forms and space becomes irrelevant.

The mountains never tell either of us stories of loss and abandonment.

Flowers grow in the most unlikely places.

The wood smells like the earth after the rain.

Something shifts forever in what we both call home.

You trace my childhood dreams in your palm, like a constellation you know by heart.

Constellations are always visible because the sky is clear every night and winter is never too cold, snow never melts completely at the very top, it is snow from last and this year, and from years before everything changed.

Look me in the eye and tell me that nothing really matters.

We will always find our way home, we will always find our way home.

We plant trees in forests at dawn. We watch them grow.

"Tell me a story," I say, and you start it with a day in the 21st century. "We are the story of today and tomorrow."

I stop cutting my hair and it turns into a forest. Inside the forest, we live our own story. It is ours, we inhabit it like it's ours, we make it ours, as we see fit. The forest can't help it but grow. It is, after all, a forest, and that's what they tend to do. We dream and breathe its wilderness.

The circle of the world is whole and I am a part of it. I am inside it and it feels safe and warm. I am centered.

There is no need to focus, to keep the narrative line straight, to know where it is going.

We breathe miracles. In and out.

We fly. I, I, I. You, you, you. She, she, she. He, he, he.

It does not matter who is mother, father, sister, daughter, child. We are what we are. We are who we are.

Becoming, always becoming, always for the better.

A cube with all the colors, always fitting, never never never never never lost.

A kaleidoscope is how our life is – reflecting,
refracting, for whoever has their eyes open.
The trees are not hiding.

"Tell me a story," you say. And I say: "Fairy tales are dead, why don't we go somewhere instead?"

Language becomes irrelevant.

The roads are hours and ours to cross, nobody is there to check what happens at the border, we can touch the earth and the sky and each other and nothing else matters.

Everything is us and ours. We are the sun and the wind.

The underbelly of the world grows just like my own belly.

The Earth Mother Manifesto – A Prose Poem

I AM A mother and a wife. I am a writer and a woman. I am someone who wakes up in the mountains, before everyone else. Not to clean the house, not to write, not to prepare breakfast, but to breathe in the wet morning air.

To wander the streets on my own, to cross that bridge, into the forest, where waterfalls just are and just flow, into a river, not a lake. To climb that steep mountain path and find those trees that only belong in the forest and would always look lost in the city. To dig my hands deep into the earth – the earth that is wet, but not dirty, and so full of yet unexplored life.

I am a mother and a wife, and I know that if I do not return home right now, if I linger in the forest just a little longer, or a lot, and if my daughter and my son are no longer sleeping, my husband will be there to take care of them. And if my daughter and my son wouldn't be twins, they would still be who they are – themselves, not our mirror reflections.

I am a woman and I am my own house. My words are not broken and they are always heard and trusted. I am not my genes. Each one of us living here is a house of his or her own making. Inside the house, there are many rooms. Each room feels like a mother's womb, but the doors are always open, to enter and exit.

Epilogue

The Body and the Voice

ONCE, THERE WAS a little girl, bright as the moon on a stormy sky. Her name was Ella. Ella wasn't really a girl, but didn't know what else she might be. Ella spoke the language of flowers and trees and could take shape out of thin air whenever a tree or a flower needed her help to grow. Most often, the growing plants just needed someone to talk to. Once a flower or tree no longer needed her, she'd have to leave and re-materialize in a new forest.

Ella lived in forests, but unlike the growing acacia tree, and the old fir tree, and the wild rose bushes, and all the other plants she knew and loved so well (for despite constantly moving, she remembered them all), she had no roots, no body of her own. She didn't belong to a certain species and didn't know other creatures like herself.

One rainy day, down the path to the waterfall, Ella saw something she hadn't seen before, growing wildly in the middle of a bush. It was a tree, with a trunk like any other trunk, but the tree was growing roots in plain sight instead of branches. Had someone uprooted the tree? How come its roots could still grow? They looked like old roots, resembling human bones, and they were quickly spreading like embracing arms above the forest.

Ella placed her tiny transparent hands onto the trunk. "Hello," she said, and listened. But the tree remained silent. She didn't know if the tree could hear her. Ella returned the next day. The tree had stopped growing towards the sky, but there were some leaves taking shape on its root-branches. Two birds were sitting and kissing at the top of the tree. They were flying away now and then, always together, and bringing back grass and little branches. Ella wanted to ask them what kind of tree this was, but she couldn't speak the language of birds. "Hello," she said, placing her little transparent hands on the trunk of the tree again. The tree once again did not answer, not with words, at least. Yet she could sense the vibration of the sap moving up and down inside the trunk. On the third day when Ella came back to the tree, its trunk had widened and flowers of all colors of the rainbow were blooming at the very top of the roots. One thing was clear: this tree didn't need her help to grow.

The birds were nowhere to be seen, but they seemed to have left a nest behind. Ella flew to the nest and let it take her into its arms. There was grass up there, and strawberries, and honey jars, and a doll that looked a lot like the reflection she saw down by the river, her reflection, on days when the sun would come out and shine its light. Ella felt a wave growing from her chest into her head and spreading over and into her arms. There was water in her eyes. It rolled down her cheeks and into her mouth. It tasted like salt.

"I'll be your body if you'll be my voice," she seemed to hear the tree whisper.

"I promise to really listen. And be the voice you cannot be," Ella said. For the first time for as far as she could remember, Ella felt heaviness in her bones. Ella had bones! For the first time ever, she slept. And when she woke up, the sun was warming up their roots, their leaves, their nose.

Ella stayed with her tree for a long time. Together they wrote the story of the tree of life, whose roots grow into the sky, exposed to wind, rain, and sunshine, not hiding anything from the world. They wrote this story and many others. They never seemed to grow out of new leaves and new words. The tree became the heart of the forest. Creatures of the forest would come to them and ask them to help them tell their stories too. Their real and honest stories. And when Ella couldn't speak with them and listen to their stories, the tree could.

One day, the birds came back to the tree. They looked older and had changed colors and seasons, but they were still the same birds from ages ago, back when Ella had no body and the tree had no voice.

By now, Ella was no longer a little girl. She was a young woman with a firm body and arms that looked like branches but still had human bones, and fingers to caress the clouds and waterfalls with. She could still fly, but only at night. More birds came to her tree that week. Ella didn't mind sharing her home. The tree would tell them: "Hello, you're welcome to nest on me." And they did. Their eggs were to release new life soon.

Ella and her tree knew it was time. For Ella to leave and travel to other forests and to share their love story – the story of the tree who gave her a body when he needed a voice – and all the stories of the creatures of her forest, with other forests out there, with the world. To share it and one day, when the earth would tumble back into darkness, to let it go.

Afterword

What is happening right now inside you,
As you finish reading these pages?
Are you thinking about your own family,
Your own ancestors, your own unhealed narrative?
If you could send a ripple of love back in time,
If you could change one thing in your family's history,
What would that be?

When I first started writing this book, I thought it would be primarily a personal family story about the horrors of communism, as experienced by my family; a book primarily about my mother and grandfather, and perhaps a little about me. Maybe to some extend a book about epigenetics and intergenerational trauma. A book that would help me find new answers about my grandfather and his time in prison perhaps. This was my very first idea, and I had hopes that our 3 stories would act like 3 braids and take equal space on the page. In time, my voice took over, in search of itself, but I also wanted to leave enough room for the other voices to stand on their own, in their own words, as they otherwise never could.

I never thought this would, in time, become a book primarily about personal identity, my personal identity, covering also aspects of immigration and failed romantic relationships. I did not know it would also become a book about nature in general, and that elements of nature would end up defining its main chapters. But life happened in parallel to the writing that took several years, and, in the process, it kept adding new layers to a book-in-progress in which time and space almost ended up becoming characters in their own right.

I had never intended to write about my father and other members of our family. When I did, I tried to do it truthfully, with love and compassion, perhaps with anger at times, but not with resent, and only if it served the bigger story. I have only disclosed actual names when absolutely necessary. I made a pact with myself in terms of where to draw the boundaries of disclosure – write with honesty, covering the full range of events and emotions, and only if the event was part of the larger story. While I do not agree with some of my parents' actions and their life views, I also do not blame them for how they raised me – I believe we all did the best we could under terrible circumstances.

—~—

I often find myself looking at the little 7-year old girl that I used to be and wonder: would she like the woman she will one day become? I can only hope that the answer to this question is yes. This little girl, who has witnessed one of the bloodiest falls of communism in European history, is a shy 7-year old who likes to read and write stories, and poems about kittens, butterflies, and stars. She has experienced and witnessed some terrible things, yet she has almost always thrived. I can still feel her breathing and daydreaming inside of me. She is watchful, doesn't lie to herself, and doesn't accept what the world tells her – about herself and many other things – as a universal truth. She questions things in search of her own truth and path in life. On some days she feels despair, but she can still hope and dream.

She is able to project herself into the future and work towards the next steps, embrace the opportunities that come her way and become the person she wants to be, and then another person, and another.

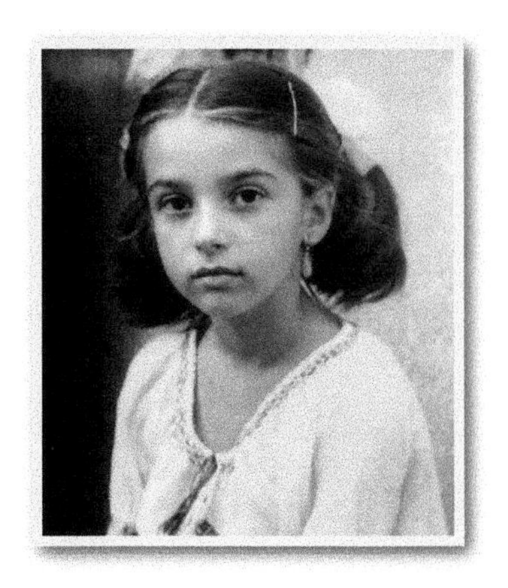

Through words and travel, she can transcend the limitations her genetics and country of birth have imposed on her; she can let her voice run wild and free and, in doing so, build bridges to inner worlds other than her own, and to the bigger world out there, to the many countries and forests of the world.

Her voice is her biggest strength. It feeds on the oppressed voices of her ancestors and everything she experiences in her travels around the world.

This little girl, from a time before things started visibly collapsing, is and will always be my inner compass. I owe her my life.

She is the voice that breaks the silence,
to speak for the unheard.
Who gets to choose
which stories we get to tell?
There's an imprint in my body
that longs to heal the family narrative,
that longs to change the course of history,
that longs for the light of the day
when all stories will count
and all voices will sing
without having to echo each other.
In my personal utopia, all voices are seen and heard.
Nobody needs to hide their true voice
or feel ashamed of any part of it.
In my personal utopia, all stories matter.
Each story matters.

Sources and Acknowledgements

I NEVER MEANT to write a book of history and I haven't. Given this, I am deliberately not including bibliographical references in a separate chapter. However, I am referring to actual events that present a story going beyond one person and one family. To that extend, in addition to my grandfather's secret police files, I have used family journals, sources available in the public domain, as well as my own subjective memory of certain events, such as the fall of communism from a child perspective.

I finished writing the full first draft of this book during the second wave of the pandemic, after my mother's clinical death. I continued polishing my manuscript for another year. The shorter version of *Our Voices* was 1 of the 5 nonfiction finalists in the *Gold Line 2020 Chapbook Contest*. Several of the fragmentary pieces included here have been previously published in earlier forms, as detailed below:

- *On the Way* in *Tupelo Quarterly* (as a finalist in the *Prose Open Contest*, which led to a *Best of the Net* Award nomination)
- *Silence(d) I* in *Poetry Breakfast*
- *Willow* in *Dog-Ear*
- *Worship* in *Munich Stories 2016*

- *if you want to know me* in *Calgary Poetry Magazine* (as second place winner in the *First Calgary Poetry Contest* and later in *World's Best Poems, Vol. 1*)
- *Wedding Picture* in *Flash Frontier*
- *My Mother Sells Water from the Fountain, The Tracks,* and *Speak as the Tree-Acacia* in *Headline Poetry and Press*
- *Disconnection* in *Feed*
- *Poetry and Nature Brought Me Back to Myself* in *The Power of Poetry*
- *I Live in Words* and *Wolf* in *Wildroof Journal*
- *The Earth Mother Manifesto – A Prose Poem* in *Arcana 2020*
- *Body (III)* in *Arcana 2021.*

Throughout 2019, before the pandemic, I gave readings with parts of the book at different venues in Munich, at the *P-bar*, the *Munich Readery*, the *Münchner Literaturbüro*, and the *Blackbox* in the *Cultural Center Gasteig*, and allowed my family's stories to breathe in the world, allowed our voices to be heard and meet other voices, from all over the globe.

The reading at the *Blackbox* (photo on the next page) was organized by *GeFoRum* and marked 30 years since the fall of Romanian communism. I hereby thank the film director Brigitte Drotlof, who told me then: "Next time we'll meet up with the book!".

Fragments of *Our Voices* were developed based on writing prompts or under the guidance of incredible mentors – Lidia Yuknavitch and her staff of teachers at *Corporeal Writing* (in particular her sister, the poet Brigid Yuknavitch), Marianne Rogoff, Jena Schwartz, Kase Johnston, Jenna McGuigan, Sarah Selecky, Jennifer Pastiloff, Tawnya Renelle – and in various groups and countries, both online and offline.

Last but not least, I would like to thank Paula Carter for her feedback on the whole manuscript; my Romanian photographer, writer, and truth seeker friend Claudia Tănasescu, who acted

as my inofficial "finish and publish your book" coach; my Iranian-Canadian friend Sara Tehranian, my soul sister; my German writer, photographer, and scientist friend, Gerrit Volkmann, who has always been an inspiration; all my early readers, who have made it easier for me to accept and open up about all my dark places as well as to release them, as old clothes that we love but which become too small and we have to let go of as we grow into bigger versions of ourselves; and everyone else who has encouraged me along the way and has helped me bring *Our Voices* to life, one fragment at a time.

About the Author

"Diana Radovan PhD ELS is a generous member of the international writing community, taking part as a teacher, editor, collaborator, and member of numerous professional associations."
Marianne Rogoff, author of *Silvie's Life* and *Pushcart Prize* nominee

Diana Radovan PhD ELS is a Romanian-born (1982) multilingual and multigenre author, currently (2022) living in the Bavarian Alpine village of Lenggries, Germany. To date, she has lived in Romania, Canada, and Germany.

She is a regular contributor at *Headline Poetry and Press*, the *Arcana 2020* literary curator, and the founder and former workshop leader of the multicultural group *Creative Writing in Munich*. Earlier, she was a teacher at *Sarah Selecky Writing School* and a reader and editor at *Flash Fiction Magazine*. She now teaches a workshop on kaleidoscopic narratives in Tawnya Renelle's online school *Beyond Form Creative Writing*.

Her writing – poems, short stories, personal essays, and hybrid forms – has been published internationally since 2004 in literary magazines and anthologies, online and in print, in English, Romanian, and German, and has brought her many awards and nominations over the years, including for the *Best of the Net* award and the *Virginia Woolf* literary prize.

Our Voices is her first book and a love letter to everyone who has lived under oppression at some point during their lives (and isn't that all of us?). It is also an invitation to her readers to seek expression of their own hidden family stories and to engage in a search for personal identity through writing, nature exploration, and other creative means.

Discover Diana's publications, awards, and creative writing philosophy at www.dianaradovan.com.